CATASTROPHE!
THE LOOTING AND DESTRUCTION OF IRAQ'S PAST

edited by

GEOFF EMBERLING
&
KATHARYN HANSON

with contributions by

McGUIRE GIBSON, DONNY GEORGE, JOHN M. RUSSELL,
KATHARYN HANSON, CLEMENS REICHEL, ELIZABETH C. STONE,
& PATTY GERSTENBLITH

THE ORIENTAL INSTITUTE MUSEUM OF THE UNIVERSITY OF CHICAGO

Library of Congress Control Number: 2008923580
ISBN-10: 1-885923-56-2
ISBN-13: 978-1-885923-56-1

© 2008 by The University of Chicago. All rights reserved.
Published 2008. Printed in the United States of America.

The Oriental Institute, Chicago

Oriental Institute Museum Publications No. 28

This volume has been published in conjunction with the exhibition
Catastrophe! The Looting and Destruction of Iraq's Past.

Published by The Oriental Institute of the University of Chicago
1155 East 58th Street
Chicago, Illinois 60637 USA
oi.uchicago.edu

Front Cover Illustration:

Looters digging at the site of Isin, January 2004.
Photo copyright Carabinieri T. P. C., Italia.

Printed by M&G Graphics, Chicago, Illinois.

The paper used in this publication meets the minimum requirements of American National Standard for Information Service — Permanence of Paper for Printed Library Materials, ANSI Z39.48-1984
∞

TABLE OF CONTENTS

Foreword. *Gil J. Stein, Director, Oriental Institute*	5
Preface. *Geoff Emberling, Director, Oriental Institute Museum*	7
Map of Iraq	10
Time Line of Events	11
The Looting of the Iraq Museum in Context. *McGuire Gibson, Oriental Institute, University of Chicago*	13
The Looting of the Iraq Museum Complex. *Donny George, Stony Brook University, with McGuire Gibson, Oriental Institute, University of Chicago*	19
Efforts to Protect Archaeological Sites and Monuments in Iraq, 2003–2004. *John M. Russell, Massachusetts College of Art*	29
Why Does Archaeological Context Matter? *Katharyn Hanson, University of Chicago*	45
Cataloging the Losses: The Oriental Institute's Iraq Museum Database Project. *Clemens Reichel, Oriental Institute*	51
Archaeological Site Looting: The Destruction of Cultural Heritage in Southern Iraq. *Elizabeth C. Stone, Stony Brook University*	65
Legal Aspects of Controlling the International Market in Looted Antiquities: The Paradigm of Iraq. *Patty Gerstenblith, DePaul University*	81

FOREWORD

GIL J. STEIN
DIRECTOR, ORIENTAL INSTITUTE

When we think of the awful consequences of war, the deaths of the soldiers and civilians always remind us that *futures* have been destroyed — the young man who will never raise a family, or the one-year-old daughter who will never know her father. But war in the third millennium AD has brought us an entirely new and different horror — the destruction of an entire *past*.

What is currently taking place in southern Iraq is nothing less than the eradication of the material record of the world's first urban, literate civilization. "Eradication" is not too strong a word; the mounds that form the remains of the earliest cities of Sumer are undergoing systematic and wholesale destruction by heavily armed gangs of looters who feed into the vast and lucrative illegal antiquities trade. The scale and fevered pace of this looting is astounding. We can only guess at how many tens of thousands of artifacts are being looted, but the sites themselves bear mute testimony to how extensive the damage has become. A tiny handful of the most important of these early cities have some modicum of protection — Ur, Uruk, and Nippur remain more or less intact — but almost every other ancient Sumerian mound in southern Iraq lies totally unprotected. For those that have not already been looted, it is simply a matter of time before they too are destroyed.

What is at stake here? There are both short-term, highly publicized losses such as the looting of the Iraq National Museum in Baghdad, and longer-term, ongoing catastrophe of the loss of the cities of Sumer. The world's attention, and outrage, quite properly focused on the looting of the National Museum in April 2003. However, for all the terrible losses — estimated at some fifteen thousand stolen artifacts that have yet to be recovered — we must remember that these artifacts were for the most part scientifically excavated and carefully recorded by trained professional archaeologists and museum staff. As a result, we still retain the priceless scientific knowledge their archaeological context: in what layer of what room in what site the artifacts were found. Equally important, we know their *association* — with what other artifacts they were found. Taken together, context and association are the most powerful scientific tools we can use to reconstruct how an ancient civilization developed and functioned. Once an artifact has been ripped from the ground by looters, that fragile and priceless information on context and association is irrevocably lost, and with it is lost one more piece of the record on how we, as human beings, developed the world's first cities, first literature, and the arts of civilization.

The looting of the Baghdad Museum was the most visible blow to the cultural heritage of Iraq. Far more extensive, and far more damaging, is the ongoing process of looting the ancient sites themselves. The artifacts stolen from these sites will never be recorded. We will never know of their existence, let alone their context and association. But the artifacts form only one part of the story. The mounds — the cities of Sumer — are the largest artifacts of their type in the world, and they are not being smuggled away; they are being totally destroyed, transformed into lunar landscapes of pits and spoil heaps that eradicate the temples, palaces, and houses of these cities more effectively than any conqueror, ancient or modern, could have done.

The world needs to know what is happening to the most important remains of Mesopotamian civilization. The exhibit Catastrophe! The Looting and Destruction of Iraq's Past is an effort by the Oriental Institute to show the public the clear evidence for the destruction of these cities, and the pillaging of their artifacts. The power of this exhibit reflects the efforts of many people, but I want to acknowledge four individuals who together developed the concept and brought it into a physical reality. More than anything else, "Catastrophe" reflects the passion and commitment of Professor McGuire Gibson, the excavator of Nippur and one of the world's leading experts on ancient Mesopotamia. Mac has also been one of the most articulate, active, and courageous voices warning of the impending crisis, and documenting the losses. Geoff Emberling, Director of the Oriental Institute Museum, has been the key organizer of this exhibit, pulling together the contributors and conceptualizing the format and content. This reflects Geoff's own deep commitment to the preservation of Mesopotamian cultural heritage, as exemplified by his presenting lectures and in-depth orientations on the importance of this topic to U.S. military personnel prior to their deployments. Special exhibits curator Emily Teeter has done an exemplary job in coordinating the logistics of putting together the exhibit. Finally, Oriental Institute graduate student Katharyn Hanson has played a very important role assisting Mac, Geoff, and Emily in this process.

I hope that visitors to "Catastrophe" will come away with three lasting impressions. First, the sections of the exhibition that deal with archaeological context should bring home forcefully how much knowledge there is to be gained when an artifact is scientifically excavated and its context and association recorded. Second, I am confident that any person who views the sequences of photographs showing the creeping annihilation of the Sumerian cities will feel a deep sense of outrage at the loss of our shared heritage of Western civilization. Finally, I hope that visitors will come away from this exhibit with a renewed determination to do whatever we can in our power to protect the cultural heritage of Mesopotamia by supporting laws to end the international trade in looted antiquities, and by supporting U.S. and international efforts to protect what is left of the Sumerian cities while there is still time.

PREFACE

GEOFF EMBERLING
DIRECTOR, ORIENTAL INSTITUTE MUSEUM

The looting of the Iraq National Museum in Baghdad in April 2003 was widely publicized in the international media. It remains less well known that ongoing, massive looting of archaeological sites and destruction of historical monuments poses an even greater threat to the cultural heritage of Iraq.

Iraq, ancient Mesopotamia, was home to one of the world's great ancient civilizations — including Sumerian, Babylonian, and Assyrian cultures — that developed the world's first cities, writing, and the wheel, and was also the capital of the early Islamic (Abbasid) empire. It is a region that has produced masterpieces of architecture and art over thousands of years. The loss of Iraq's cultural heritage is simply a loss for all humanity.

The writers in this book have all been deeply involved in efforts to preserve what can be saved of Iraq's past. And having had varied personal connections to Iraq itself, it must also be said that we feel deeply the suffering of the Iraqi people. As archaeologists, however, we can contribute most effectively to the protection of sites, museums, and monuments.

McGuire Gibson, Professor of Mesopotamian Archaeology at the Oriental Institute of the University of Chicago and Director of excavations at the important early Mesopotamian city of Nippur for many years, actively worked to warn the U.S. military about the need to protect the Iraq National Museum and has visited Iraq to assess damage and advise on protective measures. He is also President of the American Academic Research Institute in Iraq.

Donny George, former Director of the Iraq National Museum, worked in Iraq through the 1990s attempting to stop the growing problem of looting, did what was possible to protect the museum's collection before the American invasion in 2003, and struggled to assess the losses, repair the damage, and safeguard what remained after the looting of the museum in April 2003.

John Russell, Professor of Mesopotamian Art at the Massachusetts College of Art, went to Baghdad to work as Cultural Advisor under the Coalition Provisional Authority in 2003–2004, an essential but difficult, dangerous, and frustrating effort that has led to his continuing involvement in attempting to minimize U.S. military damage to archaeological sites in Iraq.

Katharyn Hanson, PhD student in Mesopotamian archaeology in the Department of Near Eastern Languages and Civilizations, University of Chicago, wrote her MA thesis on the commodification and politicalization of Iraq's looted artifacts.

Clemens Reichel, Research Associate at the Oriental Institute of the University of Chicago, is a Mesopotamian archaeologist who led efforts to construct a database of artifacts known to have been stored in the Iraq National Museum, for use by customs officials.

Patty Gerstenblith, Professor of Law at DePaul University College of Law in Chicago, has written and lectured widely on the legal aspects of the international trade in antiquities. She is also the director of DePaul's program in Art and Cultural Heritage Law and president of the Lawyers' Committee for Cultural Heritage Preservation.

Elizabeth Stone, Professor of Mesopotamian Archaeology at the State University of New York, Stony Brook, and co-director of an innovative archaeological project at the city of Mashkan-shapir in Iraq, has done the first research on the timing and focus of looting. She has also obtained significant funding to help in the continuing training of Iraqi archaeologists, and to restore libraries and computer equipment so essential to maintenance of a professional staff of archaeologists in Iraq.

It is difficult to keep abreast of all the current efforts to stop looting of sites in Iraq; the essays in this volume (and this Preface) reflect experiences of the individual authors. First, we have to recall the ongoing work of the brave and dedicated staff of the State Board of Antiquities and Heritage in Iraq, including museum staff and site guards throughout the country. The outstanding work of the Italian Carabinieri, described by John Russell in his essay, should also be highlighted. A number of archaeologists have gone to Iraq to assess looting as well as the damage that military units can inflict on sites through ignorance in the course of their base construction or other military activities. Prominent among them is John Curtis of the British Museum, who has inspected and reported on military bases near the sites of Babylon and Ur. Museums and archaeologists have also devised a number of training programs for conservators to maintain training and equipment in Iraq.

There have been a number of parallel efforts to educate soldiers about the importance of protecting archaeological sites. These include a cultural training program organized by Col. (ret.) Robert Tomasovic, Leader of Development and Education for Sustained Peace, that teaches many of the officers deploying to Iraq about the history and culture of Iraq. I have developed lectures on history of Iraq (with my colleague Michael Fahy) that include discussions of the looting of archaeological sites for this group.

The military is such a complex organization that it is not possible to reach all soldiers with a single program. It may be that soldiers learn very simple tasks (like how to clean a rifle) in the same way, but education and training take place in a bewildering variety of places and contexts. Units are responsible for organizing their own training according to a checklist that is mandated by the Pentagon, and there are multiple ways to satisfy the various requirements.

Cori Wegener has developed a training program for Civil Affairs personnel; Brian Rose, President of the Archaeological Institute of America, has taught archaeology to Marines; and Laurie Rush, Cultural Resources Manager at Fort Drum, New York, is working to have archaeological site protection recognized as an essential part of the environmental impact training that military personnel receive. The challenge for these efforts is to convince military leaders of the strategic importance of protecting cultural property — military personnel may be as interested in archaeology as the general public, but as an institution the military will not be able to do anything about the problem unless it is made a part of their mission.

This book is a companion to an exhibit of the same title organized at the Oriental Institute of the University of Chicago, co-curated by McGuire Gibson and Katharyn Hanson, and also planned to be shown at other venues in the United States, Europe, and the Middle East. The exhibit originated in a series of conversations that Mac Gibson and I have had since I became Museum Director at the Oriental Institute in 2004. With the inauguration of the Marshall and Doris Holleb Family Special Exhibits Gallery in 2006, we were able to begin planning in earnest for this exhibit. The Holleb Gallery allows us to present exhibits that differ from the presentation in the museum's permanent displays of the historical and artistic achievements of the great civilizations of the ancient Middle East. The exhibit on the looting of sites in Iraq is an ideal example of ways in which the special exhibit program enhances the public impact of the museum.

The exhibit, largely based on photographs but also including objects from the museum's collection, is organized around five themes. It summarizes results of investigations into the looting of the Baghdad Museum and updates efforts to recover the artifacts that were stolen. It documents looting of sites with a series of aerial photos as well as photos of looters at work. A central section illustrates the importance of archaeological context through several case studies that show what is lost when a piece is looted. The exhibit presents an overview of the international trade in antiquities and the ways in which it directly promotes looting of sites. Finally, we discuss what efforts have been made and what more can be done.

Among the many challenges posed by the exhibit itself have been our efforts to secure a loan, with the blessing of the Embassy of Iraq, of some Iraqi artifacts that have been seized by U.S. Customs. There are many such artifacts, often seized along with crude modern forgeries, and nothing better illustrates that this is an active, ongoing problem. As of this writing, it appears that the legal difficulties are insurmountable and that these objects will not be available for exhibit.

Another challenge has been getting very recent data on the current state of looting in Iraq — most of the available satellite and aerial photography dates to 2003–2004. We have tasked a QuickBird satellite to take photos of three sites at which looting is said to have continued, but our photos unfortunately have been delayed by other, more urgent military use of the satellite's cameras.

Nonetheless, the exhibit represents an opportunity to bring this problem more forcefully to public attention, and perhaps also to the attention of government officials and military personnel who might be able to help efforts to stop looting and smuggling of antiquities.

It is my pleasure to offer thanks along with those of my co-editor and co-curator of the exhibit, Katharyn Hanson, to the many people who have contributed to this exhibit and to this volume.

McGuire Gibson has had a clear curatorial vision and has carried it through to an exhibit that will have an immediate and far-reaching impact.

Donny George has been not only an inspiration, but also a source of a great deal of knowledge and current information.

John Russell, Elizabeth Stone, and Patty Gerstenblith have been extremely generous with their time, contacts, and friendship.

Many photographers have contributed striking images to the exhibit; thanks especially to Joanne Farchakh-Bajjaly, John Russell, Donny George, McGuire Gibson, Carrie Hritz, Matt Moyer, Roger Atwood, Micah Garen, Marie-Helene Carlton, Yasser Tabbaa, and Hamid Rasheed.

Emily Teeter coordinated the production of the exhibit and catalog, with the assistance of Tom James, Margaret Schröeder, and Sofia Fenner.

The exhibit was designed by Dianne Hanau-Strain of Hanau-Strain Associates with creativity under unusually tight deadlines.

Peter Stone and Joanne Farchakh-Bajjaly have made it possible with their energy and enthusiasm for us to realize our plans to have the exhibit travel in Europe and the Middle East.

Although Erik Lindahl, Preparator in the Oriental Institute Museum, has not fashioned the display cases for the exhibit as of this writing, I know that I will be thanking him for his usual great work when the exhibit opens.

Carole Krucoff, Head of the Museum Education Department, has contributed her editorial and design suggestions throughout and has played a key role in planning the public symposium at which our authors will speak.

And finally, if certainly not least, thanks to Leslie Schramer and Tom Urban in the Oriental Institute's Publications Office, who have now produced a series of catalogs to a high standard under great time pressures (and none greater than this one).

CATASTROPHE!

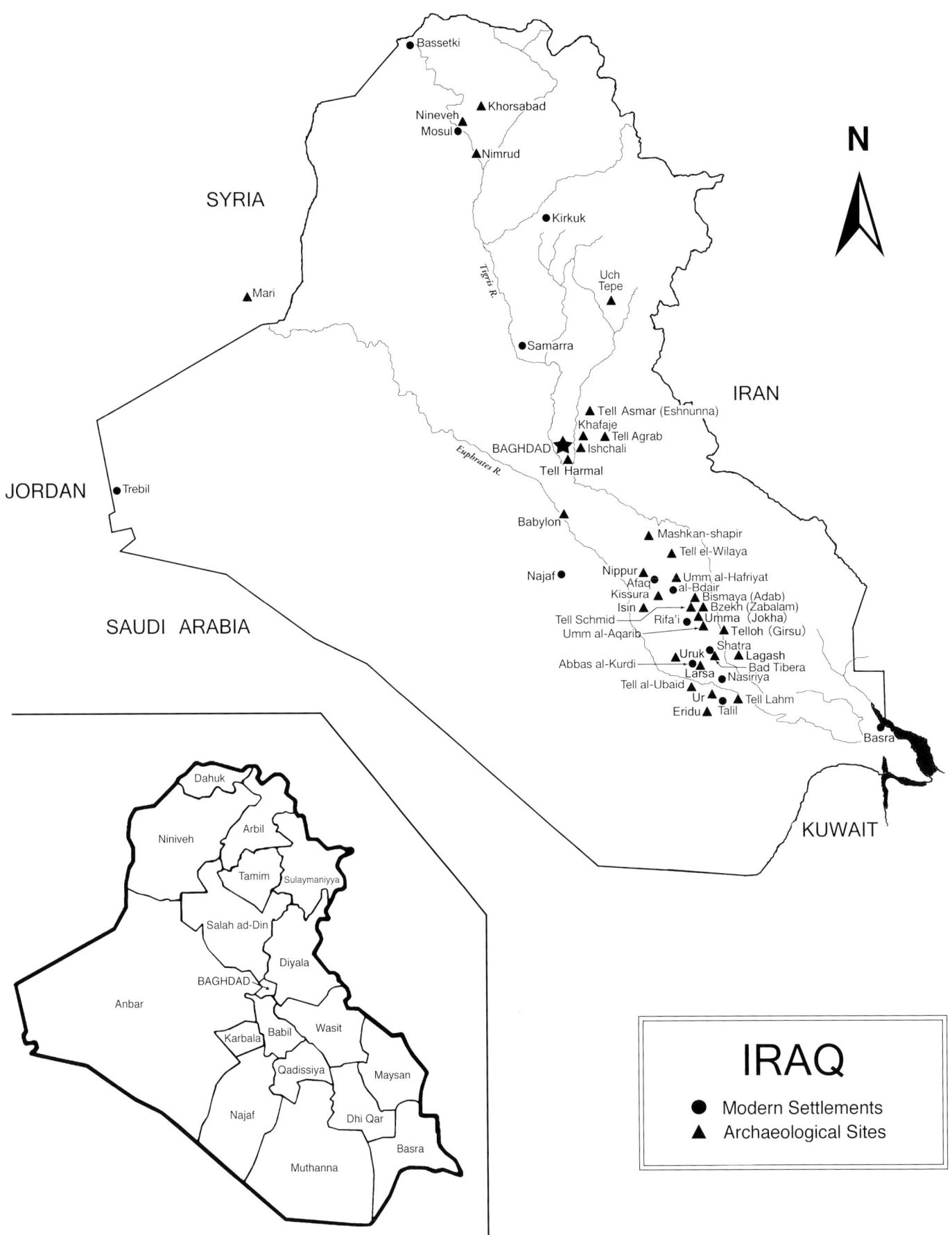

Map of Iraq showing modern settlements and ancient sites; map after Boydell & Brewer, Ltd.
Lower left: Iraqi governorates

TIME LINE OF EVENTS

2003

JANUARY

    Archaeological Institute of America (AIA) issues statement urging the protection of Iraq's archaeological heritage

24   Concerned group warns of looting threat during meeting with Pentagon and State Department officials

FEBRUARY

    Iraq National Museum closes

27   The Society for American Archaeology (SAA) writes to the Secretary of Defense urging protection of antiquities in Iraq

MARCH

early   Gallery artifacts are stored in a "secret place"; documents and objects stored in bomb shelter

6   International Council on Monuments and Sites (ICOMOS) calls on all governments to protect cultural property

19   International Committee of the Blue Shield issues statement urging prevention of damage or destruction of cultural heritage

20   War begins

27   UNESCO director urges United States to protect cultural heritage sites

APRIL

5   First U.S. forces enter Baghdad; Palestine Hotel and Oil Ministry secured

8   Iraq National Museum staff flee approaching battle; firefight in front of Iraq National Museum; U.S. tank round fired into museum facade

9   U.S. forces control Baghdad

10   Looters enter museum complex

11   Looting continues in museum galleries, storerooms, and offices

12   Museum friends and staff members secure museum; media arrive

13   Museum officials request U.S. assistance to prevent further looting

14   White House holds teleconference; U.S. Secretary of State Colin Powell issues statement assuring protection and recovery

15   Iraq Museum remains unprotected

16   U.S. forces secure Iraq Museum

17   Museum staff begins cleanup and inventory; UNESCO holds meeting of international experts in Paris, France

21   U.S. investigators begin to arrive

29   Second UNESCO meeting of international experts, held at British Museum, London, England

MAY

early	Documents and objects recovered from bomb shelter
10–12	National Geographic team and U.S. archaeologists assess damage to museums and archaeological sites
15–20	UNESCO team visits Baghdad to assess damage to Iraq Museum
21	First helicopter tour of sites to assess looting in south

JUNE

1	Flooded Central Bank vault opened

JULY

3	Museum reopens for two-hour media event to exhibit objects recovered from Central Bank
4	Objects returned to Central Bank for safekeeping

AUGUST

1	Third UNESCO expert meeting on safeguarding Iraqi cultural heritage, held in Tokyo, Japan

2004

Iraq Museum cleaned and refurbished; new security system, generators, computer network, and laboratories installed

2006

JANUARY

27	Car bomb explodes next to the children's wing of museum

FEBRUARY — Golden dome of Al-Askari mosque in Samarra destroyed in bombing

JUNE — Approximately fifty people kidnapped from bus stop 80 yards from museum entrance; State Board of Antiquities and Heritage (SBAH) President Donny George leaves Iraq with family

2007

JUNE — SBAH building at Samarra attacked and looted

JULY — SBAH representative in Basra killed in crossfire

2008

MARCH — As of publication, the Iraq National Museum remains closed to the public

THE LOOTING OF THE IRAQ MUSEUM IN CONTEXT

McGUIRE GIBSON
ORIENTAL INSTITUTE, UNIVERSITY OF CHICAGO

The world awoke on April 12, 2003, to TV images of looters running away from cameramen in the public galleries of the Iraq National Museum. What was not said was that this was the third day of looting. Shortly after came images of men looting the Central Bank, where some of the Iraq Museum's most important artifacts had been stored in deep vaults since the beginning of the first Gulf War in 1991. It was certain that there were losses from the museum itself, but there was no way of telling if the bank's vaults had been opened.

I had anticipated that there would be looting as a result of the fall of Baghdad, so I had taken some steps to try to prevent it. As early as October 2002, I had sent a letter to the State Department warning of the probability of looting of Iraq's museums, standing monuments, and sites in the war that was clearly going to happen. I pointed to the looting of many of the regional archaeological museums in the uprisings in the north and south of the country in 1991. I also mentioned the massive looting of archaeological sites in the desert between the Tigris and Euphrates rivers in the south during the 1990s. This looting fed a vigorous new market for Mesopotamian antiquities that grew throughout the period before the 2003 war.

A congruence of events had set the stage for the 1990s boom in illegal digging and trade in antiquities in general, and in Iraqi artifacts in particular. First, the world economy went into a decline in the late 1980s, and investors went looking for alternatives to stocks and other investments.

Second, the Moore and Erlenmeyer collections of antiquities, both very old, well-known, private collections with numerous Mesopotamian objects, were put up for auction. Because they were both old collections, amassed before the 1970 UNESCO Convention on cultural property (see Gerstenblith, this volume), numerous museums, universities, and other institutions that would not normally have bought antiquities, joined the major collectors in bidding for the items. As a result, the objects were often bought for unprecedented amounts. Before these sales, cylinder seals might fetch a few hundred dollars, with exceptional ones bringing a couple of thousand. In the Erlenmeyer sale, several seals were purchased for tens of thousands of dollars; three of the Moore seals sold for over $100,000.

Third, during the first Gulf War in 1991, nine of Iraq's regional museums were looted, putting more than 5,000 items into the illegal market. In the years that followed, as a result of no-fly restrictions in the south, the Iraqi government could not control the countryside, and for the first time in more than fifty years, local men began to carry out extensive illicit digging on dozens of sites. Because of the international sanctions, foreign excavators could not continue work at that time, but a few of us visited the country and heard of the damage to major Sumerian and Babylonian cities. The State Board of Antiquities and Heritage (SBAH), the agency responsible for all archaeological sites, museums, and standing monuments in Iraq, had been reduced in its funding, and as a result it had to lay off or retire many of its employees. Even when on the payroll, regional inspectors, who would normally have gone into the desert to inspect sites, were unable to do so because they no longer had vehicles.

International scholars became aware of the looting because of the flood of Mesopotamian artifacts, especially cylinder seals and cuneiform tablets, that inundated the international antiquities market. At a meeting of the Midwest Branch of the American Oriental Society in Madison, Wisconsin, in the early 1990s, there was general excitement caused by photographs of a large, black stone statue torso with a long cuneiform inscription. The photographs had been sent by a London dealer, who wanted $400,000 for the object. Because of the lack of a head, feet, or arms, the item was of no aesthetic interest. But the inscription was important, detailing a rebellion of most of the south of Mesopotamia against Samsuiluna, the son of Hammurabi. The object was said to have papers with it proving that it had been in a Swiss collection for many years. No one, of course, believed that provenance, since any Swiss collector years ago would have wanted to authenticate his purchase and would have shown it to a cuneiformist immediately, and that person would have published it right away as "An Important Historical Document in a Private Collection." A year or so after the photographs first appeared, new prints were circulated again, but this time the price was down to $40,000, and the papers with the object now said that it had been found in Jordan and had been exported from that country with the permission of the Jordanian Department of Antiquities. Again, no one believed the provenance, since Old Babylonian objects are not to be excavated in Jordan, and the Antiquities Department would not have approved the export of the object. It was in New York in the late 1990s, but I have heard lately that the stone is now in a private collection in Italy. Unfortunately, although Italy is very active in seeking the return of antiquities stolen from its territory, it is much less vigilant in policing the cultural heritage of other countries. A major collection of Mesopotamian cuneiform tablets owned by the Banco di Roma was recently published in a lavish format, and free copies were sent to dozens of scholars, including me. There is no mention of provenance anywhere in the book, although the places of origin are deduced from the contents of the tablets. The places correspond to those sites most actively looted in the 1990s in southern Iraq, including the important cities of Adab and Umma.

During the 1990s, a general measure of the increase in looting and smuggling to the international market could be derived from a study of the catalogs of the major auction houses. Where, formerly, the major auction houses might have one sale of antiquities per year, with occasionally a few Mesopotamian items, by the mid-1990s, there were several auctions annually. Although international trade sanctions against Iraq in the 1990s forbade the purchase of all items from Iraq, the U.S., British, and other governments made no move to stop the trade in Iraq's cultural heritage. You could not buy Iraqi dates, but you could buy Iraqi antiquities. One major collector in New York was heard to declare that the decade of the 1990s was "the Golden Age for collecting."

Artifacts could go out from Iraq through the Kurdish area to Iran, Syria, or Turkey, or directly to Jordan, Saudi Arabia, or Kuwait. Since the 1990s, the Emirates have become a major market for stolen Iraqi antiquities, and some large private collections have been formed there. Occasionally, Iraqi border police would intercept a pickup truck on a desert track to Saudi Arabia and find boxes of cylinder seals and statuettes or gunny sacks full of unbaked clay tablets, badly broken by the jostling. On one occasion, the guards at Trebil, the official crossing point into Jordan, searched a car with diplomatic plates and found dozens of objects. But usually the shipments were not intercepted. Once across the border, the antiquities would be taken to Riyadh or Amman or Damascus or Ankara, where they were carried by air to London or one of the other centers of the illegal trade in Europe. Upon arrival, the better pieces would be presented on velvet in chic shops or in less fashionable stalls in antique malls, and even in the market stalls on Portobello Road.

In the late 1990s, the SBAH was given money by the Iraqi government to carry out salvage projects on some of the most prominent Sumerian and Babylonian cities to stop ongoing looting. Working from that time until April 2003, even in the heat of summer, the archaeologists, protected by as many as eighteen guards per site, made important discoveries at Umma, Umm al-Aqarib, Zabalam, Tell Schmid, and other Sumerian cities. The looters moved on to other, less well-known, sites, but carried on the digging, at the prompting of dealers in Baghdad and elsewhere. It should be mentioned that there were no officially sanctioned dealers in antiquities in Iraq after the Antiquities Law was amended in the early 1960s. But dealers in antiques (rather than antiquities) and some jewelers, as well as at least one rug merchant, still had a role in the trade. After 1991, the number of clandestine antiquities dealers in Baghdad increased, but they were very well hidden. One of Saddam's bodyguards, who was also his brother-in-law, did deal in antiquities for a while, but when it was discovered, he was dismissed from his positions.

This was the background situation as we moved steadily toward war in 2003. I was part of a delegation that visited the Pentagon and State Department on January 24. There, I stressed the importance of Mesopotamia as the cradle of all civilization. I warned of the danger to sites not only from military action, but also from looting in the aftermath of fighting. I highlighted the importance of the Iraq National Museum as the repository of all records of archaeological activity since 1921, as well as hundreds of thousands of objects from excavations by Iraqi and foreign expeditions. The Pentagon people said that they knew about the museum. I also told them that there were antiquities in the Central Bank, so that should also be safeguarded. I knew that many of the most famous artifacts — such as gold from the Royal Cemetery of Ur and gold and other objects from the Assyrian Queens' Tombs at Nimrud (found by the Iraqis in 1989–90) — had been put in the vaults just before the 1991 war and had never been removed. Stories that Saddam had given the Queens' jewelry to his wives were just opposition propaganda.

Because there had been damage to several archaeological sites as a result of Coalition forces' digging in on them in 1991, I also offered to give the Pentagon the location of more than 4,000 sites that had been examined by Oriental Institute archaeologists since 1931, with the understanding that they would be put on a "no-strike" list. Later, at the request of the White House, I supplied a list of 150 well-known sites and standing monuments, and later I sent a list of more than 100 Islamic buildings. I also wrote an article for the journal *Science* (Vol. 299: 1348–49), entitled "Fate of Iraqi Archaeology," mentioning the probability of looting, pointing out the importance of Iraq as ancient Mesopotamia, and calling for the retention of the strong Antiquities Law, in event of an occupation. As it happened, the war began before the article came out on March 21, 2003.

As the war unfolded, I had some indications that the sites on the lists were not being struck militarily. But none of us knew that, on the day the U.S. troops crossed into Iraq, the looters returned to Umma and nearby sites, drove off the guards, and began digging again. We saw on TV an American general waving a tank off the site of Babylon. We did not know that as soon as the army moved north, looters arrived and looted the quarters of the Iraqi site staff, destroying plans, photographs, etc. and stealing all the equipment. They also looted a small guesthouse and gift shop, and finding the small museum empty, they burned it. Someone tried to chisel out the bulls and dragons from the brickwork of the Ishtar Gate, damaging several of them.

Figure 1. Padding installed by Iraq Museum staff before the 2003 war to protect large sculptures. Photo courtesy of McGuire Gibson

When news reports made it clear that the U.S. troops were approaching Baghdad, I sent e-mails to the Pentagon reminding them of the National Museum and the Central Bank. I knew from newspaper articles prior to the war that the Antiquities staff had moved most of the objects from regional museums, such as the one in Mosul, to the National Museum. The Iraqis thought that, as in 1991, the museum would not be targeted. They also assumed that the museum would be taken and safeguarded. A small group of administrators and staff were prepared to stay in the museum to keep looters out and to interact with the American forces.

On April 8, our news media reported that U.S. troops had reached the Ministry of Information. Since the National Museum is only a few hundred yards from the Ministry, I anticipated that the next day there would be another photo op: "General Safeguards Iraq's National Museum." But on the 9th, no story appeared, so I began to send e-mails to reporters from the *New York Times* and *Chicago Tribune*, who were in the Palestine Hotel, asking them to go check on the museum. Nothing came back by e-mail, but on the 12th, there were multiple stories of the looting of the museum. A woman who was identified as the director of the museum, and who was completely unknown to me, was featured prominently in the TV and newspaper reports. I wondered if maybe the former museum director, Dr. Nawala Mutawalli, had been replaced by this woman, but if so, it had happened in the last two weeks. In front of empty display cases, but with some objects clearly visible on the walls, the woman said, "It's all gone. It's all gone." When asked how many objects were missing, she gave the number 170,000, and that is the number that was flashed around the world. I knew from previous news reports and from familiarity with the museum's previous actions in 1991 that most of the displays in the museum public galleries would have been moved to storerooms, or were still in the Central Bank vault, so I was not surprised to see the televised images of empty glass cases in the public galleries. But it was clear early on in the reporting that some of the storerooms had been breached. I knew that there was no way to tell how many objects had been stolen until an inventory was taken. I also knew that the 170,000 figure was probably just the number that the museum's central registration had reached, and that there were many more than 170,000 items in the museum. Any one of the registration numbers might contain fifty items of the same kind (e.g., flint tools), or just one. So, when asked about how many objects had been stolen, I always said that no one would know until an inventory was done. But if thieves were in the storerooms for three days, there could be many thousands of items missing.

Later, it became clear that the woman identified as the museum director was, in fact, a former employee in the museum, who had not been in the complex for some years and would not have known of the steps the museum had taken to safeguard its antiquities. Like other Antiquities employees living in the neighborhood, she went to the museum on the 12th, when it became clear that the U.S. military was not going to keep the city under a curfew. One such employee, Muhsin, who lived on the museum grounds with his son, was able to gain the help of several other employees and bar the doors after the looters fled from the cameras that day. They put up a big sign claiming that the museum was under the protection of the U.S. troops, which was not the case, although the sign did keep the mob of looters at bay. By the 13th, the president of the SBAH, Dr. Jabber Khalil Ibrahim, and Dr. Donny George, the Director General of Research, were able to make it back to the museum, and they coordinated efforts to begin to assess the extent of the damage. Dr. Mutawalli, the Director of Museums, returned a few days later. While beginning to clean up the mess in the administrative offices, they started to assemble a timetable of the looting of the antiquities complex.

As the war was unfolding, I became involved in UNESCO meetings about the situation in Iraq and was asked to join a fact-finding mission to assess the damage to the museum and to other cultural sites. I also was asked to join a group of archaeologists to be sent by the *National Geographic* magazine. I decided to go into Iraq with whichever group got permission to go first, and I would join the other when it arrived. As it happened, the *Geographic* was quicker, so I flew with the group to Amman, where we hired vehicles and started for Baghdad within a few hours of our arrival in Jordan. We had added to our convoy Dr. Selma al-Radi, an Iraqi archaeologist who had left her project in Yemen to see what had happened to her family and to the museum. We also attached Andrew Lawler, a staff writer for *Science* magazine, whom I had arranged to meet there.

After about a fifteen-hour trip, we arrived in Baghdad on the morning of May 10, went to a hotel that we knew had an electricity generator, and visited the museum. There, we would meet Colonel Matthew Bogdanos and his investigators, as well as the troops of a tank unit in the Antiquities Library and Auditorium. We met with our Iraqi colleagues and I think that we were useful as a bridge between them and the American officials. After many months of laborious checking, the official count of items stolen from the museum is something over 15,000.

We witnessed the return of some objects, and we inspected the roughly 3,000 objects that had been returned by that time. Many were of little importance, some were fakes or facsimiles, and some items were not even from the Iraq Museum itself, but from the Museum of the Hashemite Kingdom in Baghdad (fig. 2). The Iraq National Museum, which was one of the secure places in a city that was still being looted and burned, even that long after the fighting, also had in one storeroom more than 200 paintings salvaged from the Museum of Modern Art (fig. 3).

The *Geographic* group split into two parts, one going south and the other north. I went as far south as Nippur and then returned to join the UNESCO mission. In the meantime, the *Geographic* was paying to pump out water from the vaults of the National Bank. The leader of the *Geographic* team had also heard that the Queens' gold was in the vaults, and he wanted an exclusive story of finding it or finding it gone. When the vaults were entered, the objects were found in their crates, as they had been placed in 1991. Water had damaged some of the items, and they were all taken to the museum for restoration. After a one-day opening on July 3, 2003, the objects were returned to bank vaults for safekeeping.

The National Museum was for months the focus of much discussion and the recipient of many promises of help to restore it. Unfortunately, little attention was and is being paid to the thousands of sites that are still being looted.

Iraq since 1921 has had a history of protecting its cultural heritage, especially since 1958. The strong Antiquities Law of 1936, amended twice after 1958, has guaranteed that the antiquities organization

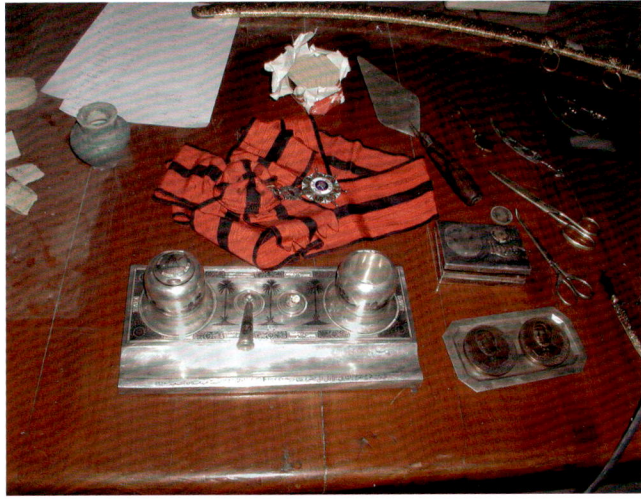

Figure 2. Objects from the Museum of the Hashemite Kingdom. Photo courtesy of McGuire Gibson

Figure 3. Paintings from the Museum of Modern Art in a storeroom in the Iraq National Museum. Photo courtesy of McGuire Gibson

had the backing of the government to safeguard museums, standing monuments, and sites. From 1936 until 1991 there was virtually no illegal trade in Mesopotamian antiquities, and only occasionally would some evidence be found of illicit digging at sites. When found, it was stopped. The Iraqis know that, in the long term, after oil revenues have dwindled, tourism based on Mesopotamian sites will be a major contributor to their economy. To let sites be destroyed and antiquities to be exported damages the future economy of Iraq, as well as causing great cultural loss. The looting that occurred at some sites in the south of the country under the economic sanctions of the 1990s, as bad as it was, now seems minor, given the greatly expanded scale of the illicit digging that has gone on since 2003. The antiquities organization has begun, once again, to send its staff to conduct controlled excavations and to stop looting at some sites, but for every site thus protected, hundreds are still being destroyed. Late in 2007, there was a sale at Sotheby's in New York, in which one small lion statue brought $57 million. Since it came from the international antiquities market in the 1940s the piece is of unknown provenance. It appears to date to about 3200 BC and is usually judged to be of southwest Iranian origin. In the news reports, unfortunately, it was said to have been found near Baghdad. But that is only dealer talk. No one knows where it was found. Following the sale, newspaper and magazine stories quoted antiquities dealers in New York and elsewhere urging investors to take up antiquities as an investment in shaky market conditions. In all that coverage, no one said that the antiquities market is almost entirely based on theft and international smuggling, and that buyers are in fact receiving stolen goods. *Fortune* magazine is preparing an article on antiquities as the newest area of investment. This one sale will cause a spike in illicit digging not just in Iraq, but also in many other countries. No site in Iraq or anywhere else is safe, and no museum anywhere is safe. The Internet has spread the word that even tiny antiquities can bring huge profits, and although the poor farmer who works all day and sometimes all night digging in an ancient mound will only get a few dollars for such an item, he will still dig hoping to strike it rich or at least feed his family. We cannot blame the diggers, but we can blame the agents of dealers, the smugglers, the dealers in elegant shops in New York, London, Berlin, or Tokyo, the collectors, and the museum curators and academics who abet the destruction of Iraq's cultural heritage sites and the theft of its national treasure.

Unfortunately, some of our colleagues do aid dealers and collectors in authenticating items, thus giving the objects more value. Even when museums will not buy an item with a dubious origin, they often still show them as "on loan from the collection of Mr. X," once again authenticating and giving more value to the objects. Dealers, curators, and even some of our colleagues say that original context does not matter, that the artifact itself gives us all or most of the information we need. They think that a keen aesthetic sense or an insight into the mind of the author of a written document is all that is needed to make the object speak. But anyone who has worked in archaeology knows that context is all-important, and that when an object is ripped out of its findspot, it loses an extraordinary amount of potential information.

An object found on the floor of a particular room in a particular building not only helps to date the building, or the building to date the object, but also helps us understand the function of both object and findspot. Objects found together can tell us a great deal about how they functioned together, and how the space in which they were found may have been used. Cuneiform tablets found in an archive may be of very different kinds, but their proximity to one another implies a relationship that would not be evident otherwise. The organizational principles behind the archive, if discovered, can even give a glimpse into the mind of the archive keeper. Any chance for such discoveries is lost for objects without provenance. And it is the culture behind the object, the mind that created the artifact, that is the central focus for archaeological research. Objects without provenance are really just knickknacks. Beautiful and intriguing, but still knickknacks.

THE LOOTING OF THE IRAQ MUSEUM COMPLEX

DONNY GEORGE, STONY BROOK UNIVERSITY, WITH
McGUIRE GIBSON, ORIENTAL INSTITUTE, UNIVERSITY OF CHICAGO

Although most media attention has been given to looting in the Iraq National Museum, it should be emphasized that the museum is only part of a larger antiquities complex in Baghdad. Besides the National Museum and its administrative offices, labs, storage rooms, and workrooms, there is also an entire wing of administrative offices for the State Board of Antiquities and Heritage (SBAH), which oversees all archaeological sites and museums in Iraq. All staff of all museums or local offices, as well as all site guards, are hired by the SBAH and their pay and pensions are administered there. The president of the SBAH at the time of the looting, Dr. Jabber Khalil Ibrahim, was the top executive, with authority over all the museums and several directorates. All archaeological surveys and excavations are overseen in these offices, and records of all excavations, whether Iraqi or foreign, are housed there. All objects found in such excavations, or seized from illicit dealing, or bought from individuals, or donated, are housed in the museum. The entire 11 acre antiquities complex occupies a triangular area in a prominent part of west Baghdad, next to the railway station and near three ministries.

On April 8, 2003, only five antiquities staff were left in the complex. All but one of the fifty guards had gone, abandoning their uniforms and even some guns. With the one remaining guard were Dr. Jabber and myself, as well as a staff employee named Muhsin and his son Ali. (Sad news came

Figure 1. View of a U.S. tank outside a reconstructed Assyrian gate at the entrance to the children's section of the Iraq National Museum. The gaping hole in its facade was made by a U.S. tank round. Photo courtesy of Joanne Farchakh-Bajjaly

Figure 2. Museum officials attempted to secure the basement by blocking the doorway with a wall of cinder blocks. However, sometime between April 10 and 12, 2003, looters breached the doorway, allowing them access to areas in which some of the most precious artifacts were stored. Photo courtesy of McGuire Gibson.

from Baghdad in January 2008 that Muhsin and Ali were killed in an attack on their house in Saydiya, Baghdad.) Dr. Nawala Mutawalli, the director of all museums, including the Iraq Museum, had left the day before. We intended to stay in the basement of the museum, and we had stockpiled enough food and water there to last two weeks. But when Dr. Jabber heard helicopters very close and saw four or five men in black uniforms leap over the fence into the museum's front garden with RPGs in their hands, he came and told us that a battle was about to take place and that everyone should leave by the back gate. After locking all the outer doors, we left. Muhsin and his son went to their house at the rear of the museum grounds. Dr. Jabber and I drove across a bridge to the east side of the Tigris River, where we stayed in a building belonging to the antiquities service. We intended to return to the museum in a few hours, when the expected battle would be over. As it happened, U.S. troops closed all the bridges and no one was allowed to cross for five days.

The battle at the National Museum lasted a very short time. One large round hole in the top part of the ornamental Assyrian gateway that leads to the Children's Museum (fig. 1) and a trail of blood down the steps inside it were the only real signs of the battle. Subsequent examination of the garden area by McGuire Gibson in May 2003 revealed that only one or possibly two small-caliber bullets had hit the front walls of the museum, and not one window was broken. Clearly, the four or five black-clad men had not put up much of a fight. At the rear of the complex, one 50 mm round pierced the wall of a second-floor storeroom, near a window that was later said to be a sniper's nest. But that window allowed a view only of blank walls and one small, black metal door in a wall of the museum; the sniper would have had very little to shoot at. Beyond that small door, there is a major street at the rear of the antiquities complex. The damage to stores and colonnades on the opposite side of the street and large chunks taken out of stone columns showed that there had been a real battle there. But on the near side of the street, the high outer wall of the antiquities complex showed no more than forty small-caliber bullet holes, mostly around the small, black metal door, the only entrance to the complex on that side. The wall of the antiquities complex had no place for fighters to take cover, other than that small doorway, and only one man at a time could use it. So, the battle was fought across the street, opposite the museum. It was through this small door that Dr. Jabber and I had left on the 8th. This door is laughable as a museum door, given that it is completely open at the top, allowing anyone to climb over it. In normal times, the museum guards, whose housing was just inside the door, would have prevented anyone from entering. The small door allowed the guards to go shopping for food or visit the adjacent mosque. But this was not a normal time, and it was through this door that some of the looters entered the complex.

From the afternoon of the 8th of April, and all of April 9th, nothing happened at the antiquities complex. As in all of Baghdad, people expected marshal law and a curfew, so they stayed in their homes. The U.S. Army had tanks at the intersection about 50 meters west of the museum entrance and at another intersection to the east, about 150 meters away.

On April 10th, the first group of looters entered, probably through the small back door. It has been concluded that this was a group of professional thieves who had some information on the location of highly prized antiquities. They broke through a sealed, bricked-in window of a museum hall and then went through a set of halls to a doorway that gave access to the underground storerooms. They broke through a metal grate, went downstairs, and opened a metal door, only to find that the doorway had been sealed with cinder blocks. The men broke through the wall and went down more stairs in the dark, since there was no electricity (fig. 2). There is evidence that the looters picked up plastic packing material to burn as torches as they passed through two storerooms full of pottery and other objects to reach the back wall of another room, where there was a bank of metal safes and locked cabinets. Here was stored a famous collection of Islamic coins, as well as thousands of cylinder seals and jewelry of early historical periods. They knew where to find the keys to the cabinets, and had they used them immediately, the losses from the museum would have been even more devastating than they were. As it was, they first examined a set of plastic boxes that were stacked there, but they did not even check a large number of empty cardboard boxes on top of the cabinets. The plastic boxes contained items that had been sent out to European museums for exhibitions in the 1980s. The objects were still not locked away because the museum had bought new safes, but the keys had not been included in the shipment. The looters took down the plastic boxes and threw away the wrappings, taking approximately 5,000 cylinder seals and 5,000 pieces of jewelry. In their haste, the looters lost the cabinet keys in one of the boxes on the floor, and, probably because of the lack of light, they did not find them. Thus, the coin collection and the rest of the seals were not stolen.

It is not clear if this group of thieves took anything from the public galleries. Another set of looters arrived later that day, coming in from the immediate neighborhood and entering any available door. The U.S. troops did nothing to stop them. Muhsin went out to the American tanks twice to try to get them to move to the front of the museum, but after checking with commanders, the tank crews said that they had to stay at the intersection. This second group of looters was more interested in furniture and electronic equipment than in antiquities. They broke through 120 wooden doors of administrative and research offices, labs, and records rooms in the antiquities complex (fig. 3). They carried off desks, chairs, tables, drapes, computers, fans, air conditioners, electrical fixtures, and even the building's wiring. They did not take

Figure 3. One of the most devastating blows to the future understanding of archaeology in Iraq was the vandalism, and in some cases destruction, of the museum's archives. It will take years to restore the museum's institutional memory. Photo courtesy of Joanne Farchakh-Bajjaly

Figure 4a. The Warka vase, a masterpiece of Sumerian art. Excavated at Uruk (biblical Erech, modern Warka; ca. 3500–3000 BC). Photo copyright Scala / Art Resource

Figure 4b. When looters stole the Warka vase, they toppled the display case and hacked the ancient vessel away from its reconstructed base. Photo courtesy of John M. Russell

Figure 5. The Bassetki statue base of the Akkadian period (ca. 2300 BC) was found coated in axle grease and submerged in a cesspool outside a Baghdad house. Photo courtesy of Donny George

file cabinets, but they did scatter their contents up and down the halls and tried to set fire to the building using piles of paper records. The public galleries attracted them, and they ripped thirty-four artifacts off the walls and out of display cases. The members of the museum staff who had been chosen to take down the displays and hide them in the last weeks before the war had left in place all the large-scale objects, such as Assyrian stone relief slabs and some artifacts affixed to the walls. They also put down sandbags in front of the reliefs to lessen the damage if they toppled from bomb blasts. (The antiquities complex was not bombed, presumably because it was on a no-target list.) Unfortunately, due to lack of time and equipment, the staff members doing the removal of objects also decided to leave a few very heavy or very fragile items on display, thinking that looters would be unlikely to move things that heavy. Among the artifacts left on display were the famous Warka vase (fig. 4), the Bassetki statue base (fig. 5), and the statue of Entemena, all of which were stolen. It was probably the Bassetki statue base, made of copper and weighing more than 300 pounds, that caused the breaking of every step in the marble staircase as it was dragged from the mezzanine gallery to the ground floor (fig. 6).

The mob opened one of the storerooms on the ground floor and ransacked it, taking things without

Figure 6. Staircase leading from the upper story of the museum, its steps chipped by the weight of dragging a heavy object from the gallery. Photo courtesy of McGuire Gibson

Figure 7. Above, bull-headed lyre (ca. 2800 BC) as restored after excavation from the Royal Cemetery of Ur (© Scala / Art Resource). Below, remains of the lyre as left by looters Photo courtesy of John M. Russell

discrimination. They also found the Ur lyre in a workroom, where it had been taken for conservation. They tore the gold from it, leaving it in pieces (fig. 7). Someone also found the Warka marble mask, perhaps of the goddess Inanna, which was on its way to the secret storeroom, but did not make it there (fig. 8). We will probably never know how many items were taken from the ground floor storeroom, because it had not yet been inventoried. It is especially difficult to conduct an inventory in this room because it is not organized by Iraq Museum (IM) numbers, but by site and by the numbers given to the items by the excavators. Over the past seventy years, since the founding of the museum, the museum staff has determined that most pieces brought back from excavations are not likely ever to be exhibited. Although an item may be of great importance for archaeologists, since it gives evidence of date or function of a grave or building, its broken or damaged condition keeps it from being displayed. To take inventory of this room the museum staff would have to take the original excavators' records, check them against the museum's central register to see which objects had not been given IM numbers, and then check each shelf to see what was there. Since the looters smashed a lot of things in the storeroom, and since objects, through the years, might have lost their number tags, it would take a great deal of time and energy to do the inventory, and there would still be numerous objects that could not be identified. For the first two years after the war, there was no air conditioning in this room and the security situation in Baghdad often made it impossible for the long-suffering staff to reach the museum. So, little progress was made on this room. Later, the museum and especially the storerooms were sealed and it is not clear when they will be opened again.

The looting stopped on the 12th of April, after international journalists arrived to document what was occurring. As the looters fled, a few antiquities employees living nearby came into the complex and shut the doors. They also hung up a large sign saying that the buildings were under the control of the Americans, which kept the mob at bay. The next day, Dr. Jabber and I were able, finally, to cross a bridge and reach the museum.

Although the United States finally did send troops to guard the museum on the 16th of April, the basement storerooms were not entered until after U.S. Marine Colonel Matthew Bogdanos arrived with a team of investigators on April 21st. The inventory began shortly thereafter. In the following two months, several thousand items were returned to the museum, many of them fakes or reproductions, but some of them very important items. The fact that scholars at Chicago and in Britain and elsewhere had posted pictures of the most important objects housed in the Iraq National Museum on Web sites made it impossible for the thieves to sell some of them (see Reichel, this volume). Therefore, they did return the Warka vase and a group of U.S. military police with some Iraqi police were able to recover the Warka mask and the Bassetki statue base in or

Figure 8. In September 2003 the Warka mask (ca. 3000 BC) was found on a farm north of Baghdad buried under 15 centimeters of dirt. Photo courtesy of Donny George

near Baghdad. More recently, the Entemena statue has been recovered by New York Customs and is now in the Iraqi Embassy in Washington, D.C.

The looting of the Iraq Museum became an international sensation, but it died as a story rather suddenly. Late in June 2003, I made a statement that the number of losses from the museum had been exaggerated and that about thirty-four objects had been taken from the public galleries. I went on to say that the inventory was ongoing, and that it was sure that thousands of objects were missing, although not 170,000, as had previously been reported. Some columnists in the United States and Britain had a field day, reporting only part of this statement and attacking the museum staff and some of the foreign archaeologists, including Professor Gibson, who were accused of making up the whole thing. With the one-day "opening of the museum" on July 3, 2003, to show off the Assyrian Queens' gold and a few other items that had been recovered from the flooded vaults of the Central Bank, the "story" was officially dead. As far as the public was concerned, the museum had been restored, and the losses were negligible. No one needed to know that right after the opening, the objects were put right back into the bank vaults and the museum was still in a shambles, requiring many months to bring it and the antiquities offices back to operation. In fact, as of early 2008, the museum is still closed and is unlikely to reopen for some time to come.

In the face of charges that Iraqis did not take enough care of their heritage, and that the objects would be far better in museums and private collections elsewhere (thus justifying the illegal market), we can elaborate on a number of issues: The Iraqi antiquities organization did try to safeguard the objects, including bringing many of them to Baghdad from outlying museums, thinking they were safer there. We took almost all portable objects off display and put them in a secret storeroom. Already in 1991 we put the most famous items in a vault in the Central Bank and left them there throughout the 1990s and through the 2003 war. We built walls across doorways and windows to deter people from entering the museum, and interior walls to hide key doors. The curators also took the entire contents of the Manuscript House, a separate building several hundred meters east of the museum, and stored them in a bomb shelter in west Baghdad. Those 40,000 manuscripts are, as far as we know, still in that bomb shelter. The antiquities organization took the most important museum records, such as the central registers, and put them and the most important library books in the same shelter. We also folded the movable library shelves shut, with the remaining books on them, and welded them so that no books could be stolen from the library. Shortly after the war, the museum's records and the library books were recovered from the shelter, otherwise the inventory of objects could not have been done at all.

The loss of objects from the Iraq Museum totalled over 15,000 items, but we cannot be sure how high that figure would be if we could gauge what was lost in the ground-floor storeroom. Approximately 6,000 items are said to have been returned, but only a small number of the cylinder seals have been recovered. Of more lasting importance to the antiquities organization is the loss of institutional memory incurred as the records of the museum and of the antiquities service in general were destroyed, damaged, and almost hopelessly mixed. Imagine if a major American or European museum were the target of hundreds of looters for three days, with its gallery cases damaged, items stolen from wall displays, its storerooms plundered, and its records ransacked. If you think it cannot happen, remember the turbulent 1960s in America and Europe.

The Iraq Museum is, for now, relatively safe, and much has been done to renovate the building. In my tenure as president of the SBAH, I took steps to make the museum more secure. My idea was to have the museum protect itself by making it difficult to break into the areas with objects. In the long run, antiquities will be safe in Iraq only when there is a return to some kind of normal life, with a government that can secure the country, promote the creation of real jobs to replace illegal ones, and back up the antiquities service in its role as the protector and regulator of all antiquities activities. In the meantime, we can all work to make apparent the illegal nature of the antiquities trade, especially in the United States where ancient objects are being seen as a desirable new area of investment. We can press governments to adhere to international agreements on cultural heritage, and we can try to extend the present U.S. ban on the import and trade in Iraqi antiquities. If the market were diminished, the supply would also be reduced, and poor Iraqis would return to less arduous work than digging for antiquities.

EFFORTS TO PROTECT ARCHAEOLOGICAL SITES AND MONUMENTS IN IRAQ, 2003-2004

JOHN M. RUSSELL
MASSACHUSETTS COLLEGE OF ART

The following account is based largely on my own experiences with implementing a site-protection plan for Iraq while I was serving as Deputy Senior Advisor for Culture for the Coalition Provisional Authority, from September 2003 to June 2004. Much of the information cited comes from personal experience and unpublished sources. I apologize for the omission of any initiatives of which I was unaware.

Iraqi Efforts Prior to April 2003

In the early 1990s, Iraq's State Board of Antiquities and Heritage (SBAH), like all of Iraq, was suffering from the effects of the economic hardships caused both by debts from the war with Iran and by comprehensive sanctions ordered by the United Nations in response to the invasion of Kuwait. The Oil-for-Food Programme had not yet been established. Hunger, unemployment, and poverty were increasing, especially in southern Iraq, which tended to be the last to benefit from Saddam Hussein's limited largesse. Unfortunately, this was also the time of several high-profile auctions of Iraqi antiquities, where artifacts were purchased for substantial amounts of money, showing that there was unexpectedly strong demand for this material.

Figure 1. Jokha (ancient Umma). View of SBAH excavations of 1999–2002, photographed in August 2003. Photo courtesy of Carabinieri T.P.C., Italia

Figure 2. Umm al-Aqarib

Figure 3. Tell Schmid

Figure 4. Bzekh (ancient Zabalam)

All images are views of 1999–2002 SBAH excavations, photographed in August 2003. Photos courtesy of Carabinieri T.P.C., Italia

EFFORTS TO PROTECT ARCHAEOLOGICAL SITES AND MONUMENTS IN IRAQ, 2003–2004

According to Donny George, former Director General of the Iraqi Museums and former Chairman of the SBAH, reports of looting at major Sumerian sites in southern Iraq began to emerge in 1994–1995.[1] Hardest hit was the northern region of ancient Sumer, the area now in northwestern Dhi Qar, southeastern Qadissiya, and southwestern Wasit governorates. Formerly part of the Sumerian "Heartland of Cities," this area was densely settled in antiquity and the early Islamic period, until the shifting course of the Euphrates River left it a wasteland, sparsely populated and subject to wandering fields of dunes. In this congenial setting, looters operated with impunity, apparently unhindered by Saddam's security forces, and perhaps in some cases aided by members of his family and inner circle.

The modern towns most central to this area are al-Fajr (Dhi Qar governorate) and al-Bdair (Qadissiya governorate), which rapidly became the antiquities-smuggling hubs of Iraq. From al-Fajr, al-Bdair, and neighboring towns, smuggling routes branched out to the markets of Europe, Japan, the Gulf, and, most important, the United States. It will forever be considered a marvel, I think, that at the same time that the United States was enforcing against Iraq the most rigorous sanctions regime in history — sanctions so severe that they lacked even the otherwise standard exemption for "informational material" — tens of thousands of previously undocumented Iraqi antiquities were sold openly on the U.S. market. Newly surfaced Iraqi artifacts were sold in the United States at venues to accommodate every price range: the major New York auction houses, brick-and-mortar galleries, online virtual galleries, and the burgeoning, anonymous, unregulated mega-market of eBay. Major public and private collections of Iraqi antiquities were built in the United States and worldwide at this time. And through it all, I do not know of a single case in the 1990s where U.S. law enforcement questioned any of these sales.

It was a perfect storm for the market in Iraqi antiquities: new market demand backed by virtually unlimited capital in the West, poverty and the opportunity to loot and smuggle in southern Iraq, the rise of the Internet with its no-questions-asked anonymity and the dime-store economics of turning thousands of small transactions into major profits, and utter indifference on the part of law-enforcement agencies everywhere. The market boomed.

Because archaeological site looting was almost unknown in Iraq prior to 1990, the site guards employed by SBAH were spread thin, with a single guard often responsible for monitoring several neighboring sites. They served primarily as watchmen responsible for reporting violations, which mainly consisted of encroaching agricultural fields and new building construction. They were neither organized nor equipped to repulse large gangs of armed looters. When the looters came in force, the SBAH guards had no choice but to stand aside. Understaffed, underfunded, and lacking vehicles, the SBAH was in no condition to take on a major looting crisis. Initially, there was little that the resources-strapped antiquities organization was able to do in response. By the time the SBAH began to receive funding to rebuild, starting in 1998 and coinciding with dramatic increases in the United Nations-mandated quotas on Oil-for-Food sales, the looters were operating at will in southern Iraq, plundering hundreds of sites.

Because the looters lived in the area of the sites, they were always present. If the SBAH sent forces to one site, the looters could move to another until the SBAH departed. The SBAH therefore determined that the only effective response would be to establish a substantial permanent presence in the area, in the form of year-round archaeological excavations at the largest sites. In 1999, the SBAH initiated excavations at three sites: Jokha (ancient Umma), Umm al-Aqarib, and Tell el-Wilaya, and added two more in 2000: Tell Schmid and Bzekh (ancient Zabalam) (figs. 1–4). Workers were hired from the local population and chosen with the goal of spreading the jobs around, so that families that

---

[1] Donny George. "Umm al-Aqarib." Public lecture, Semitic Museum, Harvard University, Cambridge, Massachusetts, October 7, 2003.

had relied on looting would now benefit from the legal excavations. Because the surfaces of these sites were already heavily cratered by looting, the SBAH trenches were often located directly atop plundered areas, and then excavated down through the pits to the less disturbed architectural layer below. The archaeological results were often spectacular, and the looting at these sites ceased entirely. I do not know if the presence of SBAH teams at these selected major sites resulted in a reduction of looting overall in southern Iraq, or if the looters simply continued elsewhere. Certainly there was no noticeable reduction of undocumented Iraqi antiquities offered on the U.S. market during this period, so I suspect the looting continued at other sites.

The SBAH excavations were maintained through November 2002, when the teams halted to prepare their annual financial reports. Because of the impending Coalition invasion of Iraq, none of the excavations were resumed in 2003. With the abandonment of the SBAH excavations the looters returned to the major sites, and following the collapse of the Iraqi government they redoubled their efforts. According to local sources, large-scale looting of sites in southern Iraq resumed as soon as the Coalition armies crossed the Iraqi border from Kuwait. In mid-May 2003, a helicopter reconnaissance mission arranged by Ambassador Piero Cordone, the Senior Advisor for Culture for the Coalition Provisional Authority, encountered groups of dozens and even hundreds of looters actively digging at sites in Dhi Qar and Qadissiya governorates in southern Iraq. The few guards employed by the SBAH to protect these sites lacked weapons, vehicles, and communication equipment and were no match for

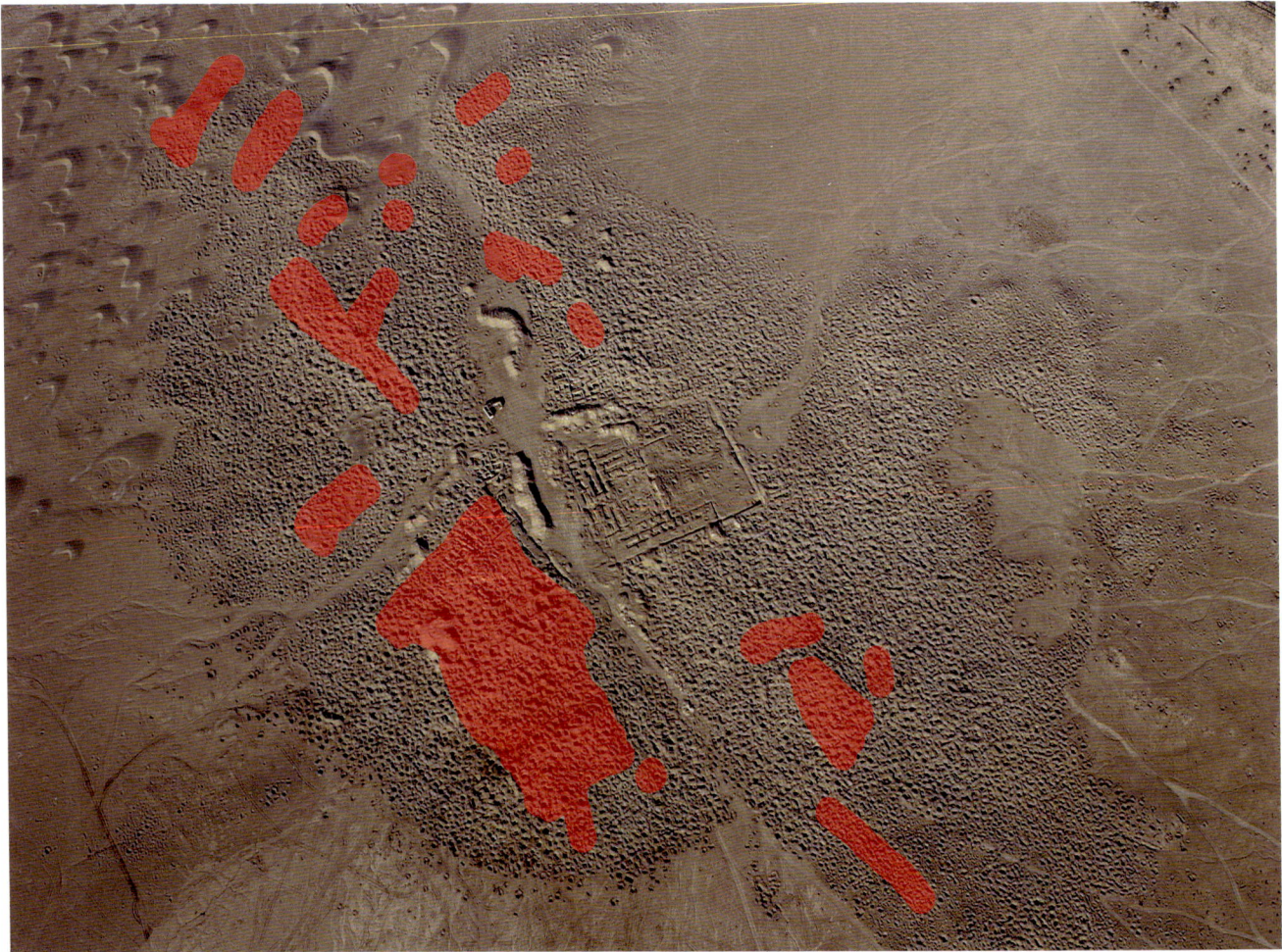

Figure 5. Jokha (ancient Umma), aerial view from August 2003, with looted areas from satellite image of December 2000 shaded red. Photo courtesy of Carabinieri T. P. C., Italia; shading added by author

these armies of looters. A satellite image of Jokha from December 2000, which documents the extent of looting prior to the SBAH excavations, shows looting pits confined mainly to the highest mounded areas. A helicopter image from August 2003 shows the looted area quadrupled, with craters everywhere (fig. 5).[2]

Any capability of the SBAH to protect Iraq's sites ended on April 10, 2003, when the SBAH administrative offices in Baghdad, which are in the same complex as the Iraq Museum, were looted along with the museum. In common with all other Iraqi state institutions, the SBAH suffered from the total breakdown of the Iraqi administration in the wake of the Coalition invasion of Baghdad. The physical damage to its offices and the theft of furniture, equipment, and vehicles meant that employees brave enough to come to work could not do their jobs. Because there was no telephone service, the SBAH was unable to communicate with its governorate offices, which were in turn unable to communicate with their employees. The theft of government vehicles throughout the country left the SBAH staff unable to monitor the sites. The SBAH was unable to pay its employees, as the Ministry of Finance had ceased to function and there was no source of funds. The evaporation of the Iraqi police and the dissolution of the Iraqi army by the Coalition eliminated the only Iraqi organizations with the capability to enforce Iraq's antiquities laws.

As the occupying power and as the only force in Iraq capable of maintaining order, the Coalition had the legal and moral responsibility to protect Iraq's cultural heritage, including its archaeological sites. Of the Coalition partners, only the United States had sufficient numbers of troops and helicopters in Iraq to carry out this duty on a large enough scale to control the problem. That U.S. forces had the potential to make a difference in the looting was shown by a group of American Marines based at the town of Shatra, midway between Nasiriya and Jokha. In May 2003, the chief archaeologist of Dhi Qar asked the Marine commander to help protect the sites. The Marines sent a patrol to Umma and arrested sixty looters, following up with regular patrols to the sites in the area to be sure the looters did not come back. The Marines maintained these patrols until they were transferred out of the area in early June, leaving instructions for the Iraqi police to continue the patrols.[3]

It must be stressed that had any senior U.S. military or civilian commander given the order to disrupt the archaeological looting, the problem could readily have been brought under control with a relatively small commitment of military resources. As we will see, the Italian Carabinieri proved that. Unfortunately, U.S. commanders and their civilian bosses considered archaeological looting to be an Iraqi problem and provided no assistance in controlling the crisis. An Iraqi antiquities official from one of the governorates hit hardest by looting told me that a U.S. general came to his office and asked him what they needed. The Iraqi replied, "We need help protecting our archaeological sites." The Iraqi characterized the general's response as "weird" — the general ignored his request entirely and replied, "We will help you with your food rations."

This odd attitude has its roots in the inability of the United States to comprehend the strong link that many cultures feel to their distant past. Many Iraqis, however, perceived this indifference by U.S. leaders to unchecked looting by armed criminal gangs as proof that the Coalition was not committed to providing security, and even that the Coalition was committed to destroying Iraqi cultural identity. As with so many other squandered opportunities in Iraq, the United States missed the chance to win Iraqi goodwill by doing a universally recognized good thing, namely, protecting cultural heritage, and instead

---

[2] For a February 2003 satellite image of Umma showing the condition of the site on the eve of the Coalition invasion, see cdli.ucla.edu/pubs/cdlj/2008_001_fig/figure2.jpg (accessed February 18, 2008).

[3] Micah Garen and Marie-Hélène Carleton. *American Hostage* (New York: Simon & Schuster, 2005), pp. 100–03. The Iraqi police refused to continue the patrols due to fear of retribution from the looters.

did almost nothing. One question that has never been seriously considered is whether addressing from the outset the lawlessness and abundance of cash generated by site looting might have contributed to establishing security in southern Iraq and thereby helped to create a climate that could have prevented the uprisings of April 2004 and thereafter.

THE ITALIAN CARABINIERI

During the period of the Coalition occupation of Iraq, the only Coalition force that made any significant effort to stop archaeological site looting was the Italian Carabinieri. The Carabinieri are a military police force that made up part of the Italian Coalition forces in Dhi Qar governorate. In Italy, one of the missions of the Carabinieri is to combat archaeological looting, which they do with great professionalism and effectiveness. The Carabinieri were therefore the only members of the Coalition forces who actually understood the social and financial devastation caused by heritage plunder, and they were the only Coalition troops with expertise in dealing with the problem. The Italian Coalition forces were assigned to the Dhi Qar governorate, one of the areas hardest hit by archaeological looting. It is very doubtful whether this was a factor in the choice to place the Italians in this area, but if not it was a fortunate coincidence. The Italian forces, including the Carabinieri contingent, began arriving in Iraq in late June 2003 and established their base in Nasiriya, the principal city in Dhi Qar.

By mid-July, the Carabinieri had initiated Operation "Antica Babilonia" (Ancient Babylonia), a project to assist the SBAH in Dhi Qar to bring site looting under control. The following information on the first phase of this project, July 20 to November 15, 2003, comes from a PowerPoint report prepared by the Carabinieri.[4] The project involved training, equipment, and financial and logistical support for the SBAH, as well as joint reconnaissance and interdiction missions carried out by the Carabinieri and SBAH staff. The program comprised three main components: preventive activities, suppression activities, and management activities.

Preventive activities included:

- Vigilant monitoring of the archaeological areas through aerial and ground reconnaissance
- Establishing passive defenses, such as observation towers, fences, and radio communication
- Training and arming of the archaeological guards

Suppression activities included:

- Patrols to suppress illegal digging
- Police investigations aimed at disrupting the traffic in antiquities

Management activities included:

- Enhancing the capabilities of archaeological guards
- Aerial photography to document and assess the extent of the looting
- Creating an inventory of sites
- Preparing an archaeological map of Dhi Qar governorate

---

[4] Carabinieri Tutela Patrimonio Culturale. "Missione 'Antica Babilonia.' An Nasiriyah, Iraq. Luglio–Novembre 2003." Unpublished(?) PowerPoint report, November [2?], 2003. While the report purports to cover the period through November 15, I already had a copy on November 2.

For the period July 20 to November 15, the Carabinieri carried out a number of missions, including the inventorying of many sites and aerial reconnaissance. In the process, they recovered more than one hundred objects, identified more than fifty looters, and had nineteen arrested (see table 1).

Accomplishments for the same period included:

- Issuing Temporary Weapon Cards to the archaeological site guards
- Provision of weapons to the guards at the sites most at risk
- Procuring a vehicle for the chief archaeological inspector of the governorate
- Construction of observation towers on three sites: Umma, Umm al-Aqarib, and Telloh
- Preparation of an archaeological map of Dhi Qar
- Assignment of a monthly budget of $25,000 for the support of the SBAH in Dhi Qar
- Computerizing the SBAH office in Nasiriya

The Carabinieri report concluded with an assessment of the obstacles to success: active monitoring of archaeological sites was nonexistent, no police unit was charged with protecting cultural heritage (the local police provided no assistance), and existing heritage law was not enforced. The report recommended that the current initiatives be continued and, in addition, a new special police corps be established, on the model of the Carabinieri, to protect archaeological sites. This recommendation was acted upon by Ambassador Mario Bondioli Osio, the new Senior Advisor for Culture for the Coalition Provisional Authority.

On November 12, 2003, a suicide truck bomb blew up in front of the Italian military headquarters in Nasiriya, killing thirty-three people. Among the nineteen Italian dead, thirteen belonged to the Carabinieri, and four of these were members of the archaeological site protection project. This tragedy temporarily weakened the Carabinieri's site protection capabilities, and activities were suspended until late December, when patrols resumed with a raid on Tell Lahm. The Carabinieri activities from November 2003 to March 2004 are summarized in another PowerPoint report, which also gives the combined totals for Operation "Antica Babilonia."[5] These results are summarized in table 1:

Table 1. Mission results for Operation "Antica Babilonia"

	20 July 2003 through 15 November 2003	15 November 2003 through 15 March 2004	Total
Missions Performed	42	48	90
Sites Inventoried	25	35	60
Helicopter Missions	7	17	24
Objects Recovered	101	201	302
Looters Identified	61	33	94
Looters Arrested	19	27	46

---

[5] Multinational Specialized Unit. "Missione 'Antica Babilonia.' Novembre 2003–Marzo 2004." PowerPoint report, March, 2004.

During this later period, the Carabinieri archaeological protection unit called itself "Viper 5." According to Lebanese journalist Joanne Farchakh-Bajjaly, who visited and interviewed the unit, its members were tremendously proud to be the only Coalition unit that was fighting looting.[6] They considered themselves to be an elite unit, and committed huge resources and four specialist Carabinieri trained in fighting looting to this effort.

By this time, some limitations had become apparent with the Carabinieri looting suppression strategy of using vehicle raids conducted jointly with SBAH staff and Iraqi police. One was the sheer number of sites, spread across a vast area and generally accessible only by poor dirt tracks, if even that. In October 2003, Dhi Qar governorate had 591 officially registered archaeological sites (and hundreds, if not thousands, of unregistered sites) and only 109 guards, which meant that many sites were unguarded. The Carabinieri hired fifty-six additional guards, but concentrated them at the largest sites, so the total number of guarded sites did not change significantly. If the Carabinieri made one site unsafe for looting, then the looters could choose from hundreds of others in Dhi Qar, or loot sites in neighboring Qadissiya and Wasit governorates where the Carabinieri did not operate, or loot at night when it was easier to escape.

Another problem with the Carabinieri looting suppression strategy was the ineffectiveness of the local police and SBAH guards on their own. The Carabinieri were training the local Iraqi police in law-enforcement techniques, but the looters and their tribal leaders did not respect the Iraqi police, since they were hired from the local population, and therefore were subject to influence and intimidation by local tribal leaders. The police knew that if they shot a looter, they would be subject to tribal vengeance. Farchakh-Bajjaly reported that she accompanied an Iraqi police looting patrol. During this patrol, the convoy was stopped by a tribal leader who pulled his pickup directly in front of them and demanded that the police release one of his "relatives" from jail, where he was being held for looting. Presumably that person was released.

Furthermore, surface patrols were proving ineffective because when they began to pose a threat, the looters would post a lookout to alert them while the patrol was still far off. In the flat landscape of southern Iraq, a lookout posted on top of a mound can see a patrol approaching from a great distance and use this advantage either to drive them off or flee. The SBAH guards enjoyed a similar advantage with the observation towers that the Carabinieri constructed at several sites, but only if the tower was on the highest part of the mound with an unobstructed view in all directions, and this was not always possible (fig. 6).

In response to these challenges, the Carabinieri developed a new tactic: in addition to continuing to use helicopters for reconnaissance, they began to use helicopters for suppression. Periodically the Carabinieri would conduct raids using three helicopters coordinating

Figure 6. Telloh (ancient Girsu). Observation tower built with the assistance of the Carabinieri. Photo courtesy of Carabinieri T. P. C., Italia

[6] Joanne Farchakh-Bajjaly, personal conversation, February 21, 2004.

together. On these raids the helicopters would approach the site from three directions. At the edge of the site, Carabinieri troops would slide down ropes to the ground, causing the looters to flee from them across the site. The helicopters would then fly to the opposite side of the site and land, trapping the looters between the helicopters and the advancing Carabinieri, who would capture them. The looters found these raids terrifying. Theoretically, this tactic could have been used at night as well, as Coalition troops had excellent night-vision equipment and the looters did not, but I do not know if night raids were ever actually conducted.

It had become clear that to suppress site looting effectively, anti-looting tactics had to combine great speed, huge area surveillance capacity, and persuasive force. Unfortunately, only the Coalition forces had this capability, since only they had helicopters and only they were immune from tribal influence, and of the Coalition forces, only the Italians were willing to use their helicopters in this way. Also, there are never enough helicopters, and the relatively small Italian Coalition force was no exception. The Carabinieri had to compete with other users for helicopter time and could not conduct raids as often as they would have wished. Nevertheless, the Carabinieri's anti-looting helicopter missions, seventeen over four months, were very impressive. The U.S. Coalition force, by contrast, authorized only three archaeological site reconnaissance helicopter missions during the fourteen-month occupation, and one of these was scrubbed due to bad weather and not rescheduled. Clearly, as long as the Coalition had exclusive access to air assets, the SBAH would have to come up with alternative ways to protect sites.

THE COALITION PROVISIONAL AUTHORITY

On September 30, 2003, Italian Ambassador Mario Bondioli Osio arrived in Baghdad to replace Italian Ambassador Piero Cordone as Senior Advisor for Culture for the Coalition Provisional Authority (CPA). Bondioli's highest priority was to stop the looting at archaeological sites. Impressed by the successes of the Carabinieri, he set out to facilitate the design and implementation of an Iraqi national Archaeological Site Protection (ASP) force modeled on the Carabinieri. For my part, as Deputy Senior Advisor for Culture, I had an advisory role in the expenditure of a $1 million gift fund, donated by the Packard Humanities Institute and administered by the U.S. Department of State, for the preservation of Iraq's cultural heritage. Apprised of the critical need, the Packard Humanities Institute authorized the expenditure of a portion of these funds for equipment to support archaeological site protection.

The administrative foundation for the ASP project was provided by Order Number 27 of CPA Administrator L. Paul Bremer, dated September 4, 2003, which established the Facilities Protection Service (FPS). The order defines the FPS as "an organization of trained, armed, uniformed entities charged with providing security for ministry and governorate offices, government infrastructure, and fixed sites under the direction and control of governmental ministries and governorate administrations." The order gives FPS guards the authority to apprehend criminals, to detain suspects for up to twelve hours in order to hand them over to the Iraqi police, to conduct searches of persons and vehicles, and to carry arms and use lethal force under prescribed circumstances.

Bondioli immediately began researching the process for establishing a site protection force using FPS guards, and in late October 2003, he submitted a proposal to Bremer outlining the ASP project. On October 25, Bremer approved the proposal, which called for providing FPS training to the 1,250 existing SBAH site guards, providing them with vehicles and weapons so that they could patrol, and providing police radio communication between the ASP guards and the Iraqi Police stations so that the police could be called when looters were encountered. To oversee the project, Bondioli appointed a former Iraqi Army officer to serve as commander of the ASP force, with the rank of FPS colonel. The plan was for the colonel to receive FPS trainer instruction at the Baghdad police academy, and then he was to identify and provide FPS trainer instruction to the most capable SBAH site guards from each governorate, so that they in turn could train the remaining SBAH guards in their governorates.

Bondioli planned to implement the prototype of the ASP project in Dhi Qar, so that they could draw on the expertise of the Carabinieri as necessary. The prototype plan, which was outlined in a memo of November 24, 2003, called for:

- Dividing Dhi Qar into nine protection zones, each containing a town with an Iraqi Police station
- Setting up an ASP radio base station in each of the nine police stations
- Providing each zone with a patrol vehicle equipped with a mobile police radio
- Providing FPS training, uniforms, weapons, and hand-held radios for the 165 existing site guards

The expenses for the FPS training, salaries, uniforms, and weapons would be covered by the CPA, while the vehicles and police radios would be funded by the Packard Humanities Institute gift.

Unexpectedly, the most difficult part of this project was the acquisition of vehicles. Because of the rough terrain and the need to carry several guards at once, the SBAH requested four-door, four-wheel drive pickup trucks. U.S. government procurement regulations, which covered the Packard gift, require competitive bidding on new equipment (usually a minimum of three bids). There was no Department of State procurement office at the CPA — the CPA procurement office was administered and funded by the U.S. Department of Defense, and therefore was unable to assist with a Department of State procurement. There was no mechanism to secure bids from dealers inside Iraq, who were primarily selling used vehicles anyway and were easily selling them to Iraqis as quickly as they could get them. Procurement from dealers outside Iraq was the only option, and in that case, there was the uncertainty of safe delivery, a problem that got much worse during my time at CPA.

On several occasions, we thought that we had been blessed with a windfall of trucks, only to have them snatched away. In early November 2003, Bondioli described the ASP project to a senior CPA administrator, who promptly promised forty Toyota pickup trucks that were already being delivered under the Oil-for-Food Programme. Unfortunately, those trucks were reallocated to other recipients. In mid-November, Masamori Inoue, a diplomat from the Japanese consulate, stopped by our office to see if we had any ideas for culture projects on which Japan might spend part of the $1.5 billion it had pledged at the Madrid Donors' Conference. We suggested pickup trucks and radios for site protection. Tragically, Inoue was killed in an ambush on November 30, and any chance of speedy action on our request died with him. The Japanese government did eventually supply thirty-seven vehicles, but not until January 2006. In early February 2004, a CPA administrator in southern Iraq promised $1 million in support of the ASP project, together with logistical assistance in acquiring the needed equipment. Unfortunately, the staffer that the CPA administrator assigned to this project was later investigated on charges of being in business for himself. In any event, no funding materialized and we heard nothing further from the CPA in southern Iraq.

We were on our own. Fortunately, our efforts were facilitated by the specialists in the Cultural Heritage Center of the Department of State, who carried out market research for the trucks and radios, prepared the request for bids, and placed orders for the required equipment. The final inventory of equipment that was eventually delivered under the Packard Humanities Institute gift included:

- 20 four-door four-wheel drive pickup trucks
- 15 police radio base stations

- 20 mobile vehicle-mounted police radios
- 90 hand-held police radios

On January 15, 2004, a VIP visit gave us the opportunity we had been seeking to make a helicopter reconnaissance trip over sites in southern Iraq. We flew over five sites, three of which were riddled with looters' craters. The worst was the major Sumerian site of Isin in the Qadissiya governorate, where we observed at least fifty looters at work, and many more could have been hiding. At Isin, many of the looters waved at us (fig. 7). After returning from that trip, I wrote a memo to Bremer that concluded: "As the temporary steward of our human past in Iraq, the CPA is the only force here that can act immediately and decisively to stop the loss." Bremer took no action.

Figure 7. Looters at work at Isin, January 2004. Photos taken by the author

By late November 2003, the ASP colonel had received his FPS trainer certification, and by mid-February 2004, he had provided FPS training to 148 of the existing guards in Dhi Qar. By this time, the colonel had decided that it was necessary to rethink the original ASP plan. He observed that some of the existing SBAH guards did not meet the FPS qualifications and that the Iraqi police were not reliable enough, nor were they well equipped enough, to respond when the archaeological guards called them. The colonel proposed a modification to the plan that involved forming an elite mobile force of thirty to forty armed FPS guards to patrol and respond to calls in Dhi Qar, essentially taking on both the roles of guards and police.

This concept was similar to the FPS forces that had been formed by the ministries of oil and electricity to protect their pipelines and power lines and was also similar to the way the Carabinieri had been operating, though without helicopter support. The drawback was that this plan would require hiring a new ASP force in addition to the existing site guards, and no budget was available for this. In March 2004, not long before his departure from Iraq, Bondioli solved this problem. At a meeting with the CPA transition team for FPS guards, he requested and received permanent funding to hire an additional 1,300 FPS guards for the ASP project. Now, the 1,250 existing SBAH guards could be kept in their existing duties as site guards, and the ASP guards could form mobile response forces, taking over the role that had been covered by the Carabinieri. The SBAH officials with responsibility for site protection supported this revised vision of the ASP program.

The remaining piece of the puzzle was procuring the necessary equipment. The trucks were ready for delivery from the dealer in Kuwait at the beginning of April 2004, precisely at the moment when uprisings erupted throughout western and southern Iraq. Unable to guarantee safe delivery because of the rapidly deteriorating security situation, the dealer backed out of his commitment to deliver. The trucks sat in Kuwait until the U.S. Embassy arranged for the U.S. Army to deliver the trucks on a convoy of flatbed trailer trucks (fig. 8). All twenty trucks finally arrived safely at Baghdad International Airport on June 2, 2004, where they remained parked for another two months until the SBAH could arrange to

Figure 8. Baghdad International Airport. Pickup trucks for SBAH arriving on Army flatbed trucks, June 2004. Photo taken by the author

pick them up. By that time, two of the trucks had been stolen and two more would not start, so sixteen were delivered to the governorates of Dhi Qar, Qadissiya, and Babil. The chief archaeologist of Dhi Qar reported that where the trucks were put into service, looting decreased by 90 percent.

The radios also arrived in June 2004. The mobile radios were installed in the trucks, but the security situation was so unsettled that there was no place to set up the base stations, which were put into storage. The weapons (AK-47 rifles) promised by the CPA for FPS guards did not materialize; by the time the ASP guards were trained the CPA stocks of weapons for this purpose were exhausted and the demand was far exceeding the foreseeable supply.

POST-CPA TO THE PRESENT

With the transition of authority from the CPA to the government of Iraq on June 28, 2004, the responsibility for U.S. aid projects in Iraq shifted to the Department of State. Bondioli and I had both left Iraq, and our successors in the U.S. Embassy were unable to devote the same level of attention to the ASP force, nor was any further U.S. funding forthcoming. In any event, the force was theoretically functioning in Dhi Qar and Qadissiya, where sufficient numbers of FPS guards were in place, together with some of the new trucks and radios. In practice, the deteriorating security situation throughout Iraq made it difficult to verify how well the ASP project was working.

By this time, other governments were beginning to offer assistance with site protection. In September and October 2004, the government of Italy sponsored a three-week training course in Amman, Jordan, for fifty-one Iraqi FPS site protection guards. The SBAH reports that this training was very beneficial and that these guards are now deployed throughout Iraq. In late 2005, the government of Japan funded the purchase of forty-five vehicles in Jordan and equipped them with radios for site protection. Unfortunately, eight were stolen in transit between Jordan and Baghdad, so that only thirty-seven made it to their destination. These vehicles are now deployed to all governorates except the ones with continuing security problems (Anbar, Diyala, and Tamim). The government of Japan also funded the purchase of forty-three satellite telephones for use in site protection. These were delivered to Iraq, but were not used because they lacked the necessary SIM cards.[7] The Czech Republic donated 1,000 surplus AK-47s and accessories to the SBAH for the FPS site guard force, but these weapons were reportedly detained by the Iraqi Ministry of Culture, and it is not clear how many, if any, were distributed to the ASP force.

According to the senior officials of the SBAH, as of early 2008, Iraq had 12,500 registered archaeological sites, 1,373 SBAH site guards, 1,406 FPS guards, and sixty-two vehicles. For the three governorates with the largest amount of looting, the totals are summarized in table 2.

Table 2. Site protection statistics for three governorates

Governorate	Total Sites	Number of SBAH Guards	Number of FPS Guards	Number of Vehicles
Dhi Qar	700	88	200	12
Qadissiya	646	85	89	8
Wasit	375	45	68	5

---

[7] Information on Italian and Japanese projects from "Report from the UNESCO Secretariat" and "Iraqi Government Report," reports of the Third Plenary Session of the International Co-ordination Committee for the Safeguarding of the Cultural Heritage of Iraq, Paris, November 13–14, 2007.

Although these numbers look encouraging, there are still problems. At the time of writing, due to lack of funding to build new guard stations, the existing guard stations for the FPS in Dhi Qar and Qadissiya are located so far from the heaviest concentration of looting that the FPS are unable to serve effectively as a response force. More guards and vehicles are needed, particularly in Wasit. Inadequate funding for fuel limits the ability of the FPS to patrol with the few vehicles they have. Political favoritism seems to be giving some looters immunity. The chief archaeologists of all three governorates report that looting appears to be increasing again in the area around al-Fajr and al-Bdair, including southern Wasit. There is still much to be done before the looting problem can be said to be under control.

Conclusions

Despite large expenditures of effort and funds, it is not clear that the site looting problem in Iraq is under control. Although I would never claim to be an expert in site protection, I would like to conclude with a few observations based on the experiences that I and others have had with site protection efforts in Iraq.

First, to be sure, it is an Iraqi problem, but it is not only an Iraqi problem — it is also a global problem, and it is our problem. Smugglers are not harmless connoisseurs and this is not a victimless crime. Smugglers are criminals who do not care what they smuggle as long as they can make money smuggling it. They may make money today smuggling antiquities, and tomorrow smuggling drugs, arms, bombs, radioactive material, and slaves. They look for weaknesses — political instability, war, lax enforcement — and they exploit these weaknesses, preying on the most distressed people in the world to make their profits. To the extent that we allow them to smuggle antiquities unhindered, we help them stay in business.

In the particular case of Iraq, the international and U.S. stakes should be obvious. Antiquities looting provides a ready source of cash that may be used by the insurgency, the militias, and the terrorists that destabilize the country. The free flow of antiquities from Iraq through Iran is one probable source of funding for the arms, explosives, and enhanced roadside bombs that flow the other direction into Iraq and into the paths of Coalition and Iraqi security forces. The United States especially should be seeking positive actions it can take to counter its utter failure to demonstrate to the Iraqis that the United States has any priority beyond control of Iraqi oil, and the Iraqi conviction that the U.S. goal is to destroy Iraqi cultural identity. Many Iraqis cannot believe that the United States is this dense when it comes to understanding the importance of cultural heritage, and therefore they attribute sinister motives to what is really simple ignorance. Straightforward U.S. action to stop Iraq's heritage looting crisis would be a big step in addressing Iraqi distrust of U.S. motives and would contribute to Iraqi stability.

Second, and related to the above, the United States could take dramatic steps to stop the site looting at any time. The Carabinieri, with a vastly smaller force in the country, showed how this can be done. At this point, the United States is the only Coalition force in Iraq that has this capability to stop site looting.

Third, international coordination is critical. Site protection is not an inventory of guards and trucks, but rather a system of components that work together. If some components are missing, inadequate, or poorly deployed, the system cannot perform well. The international response to date has been to try to provide the necessary equipment and training, but the poor security situation in Iraq and the frequent turnover in the senior SBAH administration have made it difficult for international donors to coordinate their contributions with Iraqi needs, or to determine if their donations have been effective. At this point, I believe that the most sorely needed component of the site protection program is an intensely focused international working group that brings Iraqi site protection specialists and international donors together, physically or virtually, several times a year. This would provide donors with real-time reports on successes and needs and would help to ensure that assistance was targeted for maximum effectiveness.

Finally, this chapter focuses on methods of physical protection for Iraq's archaeological sites, but as long as there is strong market demand, site protection by itself is not sufficient to stop looting. A comprehensive site protection solution must address the demand side of the market as well as the supply side. This is where worldwide enforcement of existing laws would make a difference. In the United States, for example, Executive Order 13350 maintains the total prohibition against the trade in Iraqi antiquities, a prohibition that began with the U.S. embargo against Iraq in August 1990. And yet this eighteen-year trade ban, backed by federal penalties including large fines and prison time, has had no effect on the flourishing U.S. market in newly surfaced Iraqi antiquities, because it has never been enforced. As long as an unfettered worldwide market for Iraqi antiquities is allowed to provide the funding for this "Iraqi problem," the problem will not go away. As long as the United States allows its citizens to fund the looters, U.S. denial of responsibility for this "Iraqi problem" will ring hollow.

WHY DOES ARCHAEOLOGICAL CONTEXT MATTER?

KATHARYN HANSON
UNIVERSITY OF CHICAGO

An artifact's context usually consists of its immediate matrix (the material surrounding it e.g. gravel, clay, or sand), its provenience (horizontal and vertical position within the matrix), and its association with other artifacts (occurrence together with other archaeological remains, usually in the same matrix).[1]

Basic definitions miss the importance of archaeological context: it provides an artifact's story. Archaeological context matters because it allows us to piece together an ancient narrative that provides valuable information about the past.

Before it is removed from the ground, every artifact has a context based on its location and surroundings. Archaeological context is provided by information about the archaeological level in which an artifact was found, the type of building where it was found, where it was found inside that building, objects found nearby, and how these artifacts were discarded. Context thus gives an artifact its story; it ties each object into the larger cultural matrix of an ancient building, neighborhood, site, or even an entire regional history.

During an archaeological excavation an artifact's context is carefully identified and recorded by archaeologists. Archaeologists measure and map an artifact's horizontal and vertical location (fig. 1). This record is then available for an immediate analysis of the artifact and for future research when new findings or techniques may expand its story. These carefully recorded contextual details become part of the corpus of human history. In contrast, when an artifact is looted from an ancient site it is ripped from its context and all its potential contextual information is lost. Looting destroys archaeological sites and artifacts' context. It can be argued that a looted artifact sold on the art market can stand alone as a pretty piece of artwork, yet without archaeological context this pretty object simply represents lost knowledge.

Figure 1. Alexandra Witsell, a University of Chicago PhD candidate in Mesopotamian archaeology, measuring and mapping stratigraphy at the ancient site of Tell Hamoukar in Syria. Unlike looters, archaeologists carefully record the horizontal and vertical locations of architecture, artifacts, and organic remains before removing anything from the ground. Photo by Katharyn Hanson

---

[1] Colin Renfrew and Paul G. Bahn. *Archaeology: Theories, Methods, and Practice*. 2nd edition (New York: Thames & Hudson, 1996), p. 540.

Figure 2. Three worshipper statues as they were found during Oriental Institute excavations in the 1930s in a temple to the god Abu at Tell Asmar (ancient Eshnunna). Photo copyright the Oriental Institute

Figure 3. The Early Dynastic worshipper statues from Tell Asmar (ancient Eshnunna). Photo copyright the Oriental Institute

Figure 4. This statue was found in a pit next to the altar of the Abu temple at Tell Asmar. It is thought to depict a priest because it lacks the full beard and long hair of the other male statues of this type. Photo copyright the Oriental Institute

One of the most substantial aspects of context lost through looting is information about architecture. Architecture in ancient Iraq was constructed with mudbrick, a building material similar to adobe in the American Southwest. A mudbrick can look much like its surrounding dirt and archaeologists often are only able to distinguish between the two by consistency or color. Because these mudbrick walls of Iraq's ancient structures are hard to identify and easily broken, archaeologists gently excavate and painstakingly record these buildings and their associated artifacts. The fragile mudbrick remains of ancient homes, temples, and palaces are all threatened by looting. Unlike archaeologists, looters rip through these mudbrick walls destroying any architecture in their search for marketable artifacts.

When archaeologists excavate mudbrick architecture, we are able to draw conclusions about the function of buildings and rooms based upon the building's plan and artifacts found in context. For example, a room that contains mainly large vessels and bag sealings could be interpreted as a storage room. Similarly, an archaeologist might label a neighboring room a kitchen if it contains an oven, ash, burnt animal bones, and charred grain seeds.

While archaeologists can better understand the function of a room based on the objects found within that context, they can also better identify an artifact's use and method of discard based on that artifact's location within a specific room. One such group of artifacts is the statues from Tell Asmar (ancient Eshnunna), which are better understood by scholars today because archaeologists documented their context during excavations in the 1930s (fig. 2). These statues date to the Early Dynastic period (ca. 2600 BC) and were found during the Oriental Institute's excavation at the ancient site of Eshnunna in the Diyala region of Iraq. The 1933–1934 excavation records detail that these statues were found buried in groups next to the altar under the floors in the temples of Abu and Sin (fig. 3).

Without contextual information these statues would only yield information for an art historical analysis. Though we might gain some textual information from the few statues with cuneiform inscriptions, scholars rely on archaeological context to identify these statues. The statues' location indicates that they were used in the temple to represent perpetual adoration of the deity as a stand-in for the individual who donated the statue. These statues were deliberately buried in groups under the floor of temples, which implies that they were considered property of the deity and thus maintained by and eventually buried in the house of the deity. The groups of buried statues are associated with the rebuildings of the temples and this suggests that the buried statues represented worshippers who were no longer alive at the time of that rebuilding. We are able to better understand these statues from Tell Asmar because they were excavated and their context was well documented (fig. 4).

The above example illustrates how context provides information about an artifact's function, but context can also give us even more detailed information as can be seen in the data provided by cylinder seals. A cylinder seal for sale on the illicit antiquities market is a beautiful object and we might even glean textual information from it if it is inscribed. So what type of information is lost when a seal is ripped from its context and commodified by the art market? With contextual information a seal can provide a wealth of information about building organization, room function, or an individual's role in an ancient bureaucracy.

One example of the depth of information good context can provide comes from the cylinder sealings of Bilalama. Three impressions of the Bilalama seal were found in the Shusin temple and the Palace of the Rulers at Tell Asmar in the Diyala region of Iraq. Clemens Reichel has reconstructed the location of these ancient impressions to illustrate the responsibilities of Bilalama himself and the level of detailed analysis possible with archaeological context.[2]

---

[2] Clemens Reichel, "A Modern Crime and an Ancient Mystery: The Seal of Bilalama," in *Festschrift für Burkhart Kienast zu seinem 70. Geburtstage, dargebracht von Freunden, Schülern und Kollegen*, edited by Gebhard Selz, pp. 355–89. Alter Orient und Altes Testament 274. Münster: Ugarit-Verlag, 2003.

Like cylinder seals, ancient clay tablets can provide written information without context, but the potential information from tablets with context is far greater. When an ancient cuneiform tablet is analyzed with its contextual information such as its location and relationship with other objects, even genealogies and building ownership can be recreated. One example of this can be seen in the fragmentary tablets from Tell Asmar (fig. 5). Clemens Reichel has researched 1,200 tablet fragments from the Tell Asmar administrative complex, digitized by the Oriental Institute's Diyala Project. His work shows that these fragments illustrate a family line of officials through four phases of the architecture of the Tell Asmar administrative complex. For over a hundred years this family was able to hold onto their powerful office during turbulent political periods and changes in government control.[3] The broken tablets that Reichel used for his study would simply have been discarded by looters. Broken tablets such as these would never reach the art market since looters toss fragments such as these away and their contextual information is lost. Looters are only interested in whole tablets with market value, from which they earn approximately $50 or less.

The examples detailed above illustrate the potential information that context can provide about an ancient society. One final example of the importance of context can be seen in some museum galleries. Today museums often receive artifacts through donations. Many museums, including the Oriental Institute, refuse donated artifacts that do not clearly adhere to current cultural property laws, such as the UNESCO Convention of 1970 (see Gerstenblith, this volume). Unfortunately, not all museums are as scrupulous as they should be when it comes to investigating donated artifacts. Thus stolen artifacts may eventually end up in museum display cases since an object held in a private collection in the United States can be legitimately donated for a tax write-off for the donor.

The incidence of unprovenanced artifacts in a museum's display also raises questions about the authenticity of these artifacts. If an artifact comes from a questionable background there is no way to prove that the artifact is not simply a fake. These artifacts' lack of context negatively impacts any visitor

Figure 5. Fragmentary tablets from Tell Asmar illustrate a family line of officials through four phases of architecture. For over one hundred years this family was able to hold onto their powerful office during turbulent political periods and changes in government control. As. 30:T.551; 8.6 x 5.2 cm. Photo by Clemens Reichel

---

[3] McGuire Gibson, "Diyala Objects Publications Project," *Oriental Institute Annual Report 1999–2000*, edited by Gil J. Stein, pp. 19–22. Chicago: Oriental Institute, 2000.

to a museum, since the museum visitor has to guess which artifacts are truly ancient and which objects are well-made forgeries.

Scholars also need to be cautious of questionable artifacts. Studies of ancient tablets and seals often focus heavily on textual evidence and stylistic analysis rather than the artifact's context. Often this is because these tablets and seals were purchased on the art market and have no verifiable context. When displaying or researching an artifact we must take context into account. The modern context of an artifact, its purchase history, and ownership are never guarantees that an object is legitimately ancient. The most effective method to determine the true authenticity of an artifact is through its ancient context, which can only be verified through archaeological documentation.

In conclusion, context is the story of an artifact: the story of location, the surrounding material, and the artifact's relationship with other objects. However visually appealing or textually significant an artifact might be, without archaeological context most of its history and authenticity is lost forever. The artifact without context no longer carries the potential to further inform our comprehension of human history; rather it represents the magnitude of information that it might have shared but now cannot. When a looted artifact is ripped from its archaeological context we irretrievably lose knowledge that could have helped us better understand both ancient societies and ourselves. A looted artifact is history stolen from all of us.

CATALOGING THE LOSSES:
THE ORIENTAL INSTITUTE'S IRAQ MUSEUM DATABASE PROJECT

(http://oi.uchicago.edu/OI/IRAQ/iraq.html)

CLEMENS REICHEL
ORIENTAL INSTITUTE

The looting of the Iraq National Museum during the Iraq War in April 2003 attracted worldwide attention; its impact not only on the world of Near Eastern archaeology but also on the cultural heritage of humanity is discussed elsewhere in this volume and needs no repetition.[1] In this chapter, I account for one of our own actions here at University of Chicago following this tragedy, the creation of an online database of artifacts from the Iraq Museum that are known or presumed to be stolen.[2]

Our concern for Iraq's artifacts should come as no surprise, since the Oriental Institute has a century-long tradition of archaeological work in Iraq. Initial work at the site of Bismaya (ancient Adab) between 1903 and 1905 was followed by large and well-funded projects at Khorsabad, the residence of King Sargon II of Assyria, between 1928 and 1935; and at the sites of Tell Asmar, Khafaje, Tell Agrab, and Ishchali in the Diyala Region, between 1931 and 1938. The focus of these projects went far beyond the recovery of prestigious artifacts for museum exhibitions — a main objective for many early excavations in Mesopotamia. In addition to temples and palaces, large domestic quarters, workshops, and industrial areas were excavated systematically and comprehensively, providing a cross section through most aspects of urban life in ancient Mesopotamian cities, their political organization, religion and cult, social networks, and administrative and economic systems. The exceptional care taken in systematically recording the contexts of artifacts, using procedures that were then uncommon in Near Eastern archaeology, not only allowed pattern analyses of artifact clusters within buildings but also helped in the establishment of a sound chronological framework for much of Mesopotamia's early historical periods. Following World War II, the Oriental Institute took over work at Nippur, the holy city of the Sumerians, which previously had been excavated by the University of Pennsylvania. More recent fieldwork includes seasons at Umm al-Hafriyat (1977) and at Uch Tepe (1978–1979) in the Hamrin Basin, a salvage project that took place during the construction of a dam at the Diyala River.[3] Objects recovered in excavations between 1922 and 1967 were divided between the Oriental Institute and the Iraqi State Board of Antiquities and Heritage (SBAH). Those remaining in Iraq found a home in the Iraq Museum in Baghdad or in one of in Iraq's provincial museums. The other half entered the Oriental Institute Museum's collection, where they represent many of the highlights of the Mesopotamian gallery. Since the 1991 Gulf War, when active fieldwork by foreign expeditions in Iraq came to a halt, our focus

---

[1] The most comprehensive overview of press reports from April 2003 concerning the looting of the Iraq Museum and its aftermath can be found on Deblauwe 2003, a Web site that I have used extensively for my work and during research for this article. Articles, scholarly essays, and other statements published after late April 2003 are also archived at the IraqCrisis Web site (see table 1). Comprehensive accounts describing the looting of the Iraq Museum can be found in Lawler 2003, Al-Radi 2003, and Foster 2003. Questions concerning the responsibilities for and possible avoidability of the museum looting were addressed by Renfrew 2003.

[2] For a comprehensive summary and technical discussion of the Oriental Institute's Iraq Web site, see Reichel 2005.

[3] Online summaries of the work at Nippur and Umm al-Hafriyat can be found at http://oi.uchicago.edu/research/projects/nip/.

has shifted from site excavations toward a more regional approach, using satellite images and GIS to find archaeological sites, trace ancient road networks, and observe changes in ancient river courses over time. The study of artifacts from our excavations in Iraq gained new momentum with the launch of the Diyala Project in 1994, a project dedicated to the online publication of artifacts from the Oriental Institute's largest archaeological undertaking in Iraq.[4]

The Oriental Institute's long-standing commitment to archaeology in Iraq explains our concern for this country's archaeological heritage in the face of the mounting danger of war throughout 2002. Such fears were by no means baseless. Following the cease-fire after the 1991 Gulf War, eight of Iraq's thirteen regional museums had been looted. As of today, some 3,500 objects from these museums are still missing. The economic embargo imposed upon Iraq after the war and the resulting economic hardship that befell major parts of the country unfortunately furthered the export of the one commodity found outside of cities — artifacts dug up illegally, unsystematically, and in large quantities from Iraq's archaeological sites and which could be sold, largely below the radar of Iraqi and Western customs officials, to a greedy, ever-growing illegal antiquities market outside of Iraq. The damage done to archaeological sites was so considerable that scholars worldwide demanded actions to curb this devastation.[5] Unfortunately, the Iraqi government's de facto loss of aerial control over the southern part of Iraq and the no-fly zone imposed by the United States after the war also meant that few effective steps could be taken by the SBAH to prevent or even discover these acts of looting. Throughout the 1990s Iraqi scholars tried to preempt the looters in their actions by conducting rescue excavations on numerous archaeological sites.[6] Foreign initiatives, which could have aided the prevention of looting and helped to put archaeological work in Iraq back to its high pre-Gulf War standards, were unable to assist due to an economic embargo imposed on Iraq by the United Nations in 1990.

Months before the 2003 Iraq War, coordinates for some 4,000 key archaeological sites, monuments, and museums were compiled by students at the Oriental Institute at the initiative of McGuire Gibson, Professor for Mesopotamian Archaeology, and turned over to the U.S. Department of Defense in late 2002 with the sole intent of preventing damage to these sites in the event of war. Though Gibson repeatedly and publicly emphasized the very real danger to Iraq's museums before and during the war,[7] his worst fears manifested in early April 2003, when both the Iraq Museum in Baghdad and the Mosul Museum[8] were looted. Both museums had survived the actual war relatively unharmed, but once Iraq's government, army, and police force had collapsed, the museums were ransacked between April 10th and 12th. Scholars worldwide were quick to suggest the creation of a Web site where stolen Iraqi antiquities could be posted, and some of them encouraged us to start compiling it at the Oriental Institute. We accepted the challenge for several reasons: photographs, drawings, and descriptions document almost 20,000 objects from our own excavations in Iraq. Images of numerous other objects housed at the Iraq Museum could be easily obtained from books at the Oriental Institute's Research Archives, one of the most comprehensive libraries on the ancient Near East in the world; its holdings not only include many rare books but also

---

[4] A description of the Diyala Project, currently funded by a grant from the National Endowment for the Humanities, can be found at the project's home page: http://oi.uchicago.edu/research/projects/diy/.

[5] See Adams 2001 for a brief summary of concerns and issues of the archaeological community.

[6] See, for example, Lawler 2001 for Iraqi rescue excavations at the sites of Umma, Umm al-Aqarib, and Tell al-Namil.

[7] "[In case of warfare] …the greatest concern for archaeologists, art historians, and historians around the world is for the Iraq National Museum in Baghdad and the museum in Mosul, as well as our colleagues and their staffs, who will try to protect the collections. Both buildings are close to government buildings that were hit by 'smart bombs' in the [1991] Gulf War. Even if they survive the bombing, any period of chaos or uncertain control during or after the fighting will render both institutions vulnerable to looting" (Gibson 2003a: 1849; see also Gibson 2003b and in this volume).

[8] Few news reports focused on the looting of the Mosul Museum, which had been overshadowed by the looting of the Iraq Museum in Baghdad. See Watson 2003 and Atwood 2003 for summaries.

Iraqi publications from the last forty years that enjoyed very limited circulation. Finally, the Oriental Institute's Web site is already well known, thanks to its online publications, numerous educational components, and archaeological news groups. Less than a week after the looting, we formed the Iraq Work Group, in which our basic objectives were discussed.[9]

In publishing data on stolen objects from the Iraq Museum as a Web-based computer database we incorporated lessons learned after the looting of Iraq's provincial museums in 1991. Between 1992 and 1996, photos and descriptions of stolen objects were published by three academic associations — the American Association for Research in Iraq (TAARI), the British School of Archaeology, and the Japanese Archaeological Mission — in a series of three booklets called "Lost Heritage"[10] (fig. 1). These booklets were intended to help academics, antiquities dealers, and auction houses determine if items spotted on the market had been stolen from one of Iraq's museums. Unfortunately, these booklets had only a limited success since they never circulated widely enough to have a real impact and they were

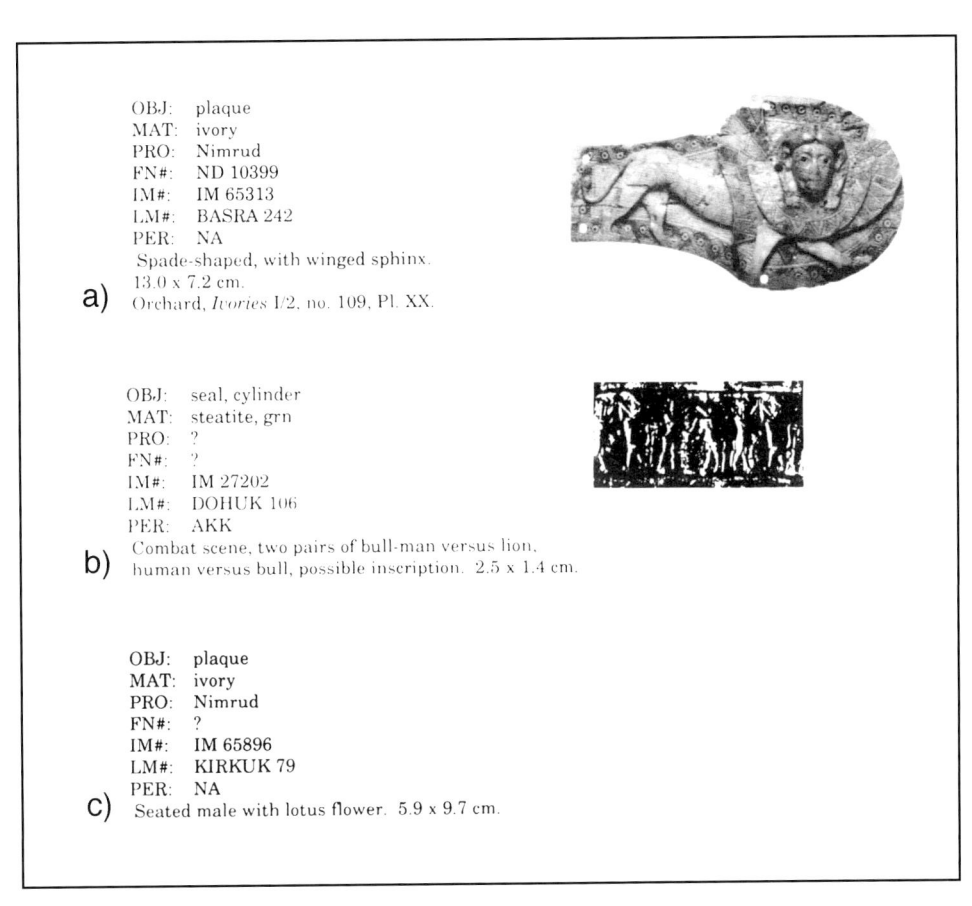

a)
```
OBJ:   plaque
MAT:   ivory
PRO:   Nimrud
FN#:   ND 10399
IM#:   IM 65313
LM#:   BASRA 242
PER:   NA
Spade-shaped, with winged sphinx.
13.0 x 7.2 cm.
Orchard, Ivories I/2, no. 109, Pl. XX.
```

b)
```
OBJ:   seal, cylinder
MAT:   steatite, grn
PRO:   ?
FN#:   ?
IM#:   IM 27202
LM#:   DOHUK 106
PER:   AKK
Combat scene, two pairs of bull-man versus lion,
human versus bull, possible inscription. 2.5 x 1.4 cm.
```

c)
```
OBJ:   plaque
MAT:   ivory
PRO:   Nimrud
FN#:   ?
IM#:   IM 65896
LM#:   KIRKUK 79
PER:   NA
Seated male with lotus flower. 5.9 x 9.7 cm.
```

Figure 1. Sample entries from one of the "Lost Heritage" booklets published after the 1991 Gulf War with a) good illustration, b) poor illustration, c) no illustration

---

[9] Members of our Iraq Work Group included Gil Stein (Director, Oriental Institute), McGuire Gibson (Professor of Mesopotamian Archaeology), Clemens Reichel (Research Associate, Mesopotamian Archaeology), Charles E. Jones (Head Librarian, Oriental Institute Research Archives), John Sanders (Head of Oriental Institute Computer Lab), and Nicholas Kouchoukos (Professor of Archaeology, Department of Anthropology). The group's work statement is posted at http://oi.uchicago.edu/OI/IRAQ/statement.html.

[10] Gibson and McMahon 1992; Baker, Matthews, and Postgate 1993; Fuji and Oguchi 1996. All three booklets can be downloaded as PDFs from the Oriental Institute's Lost Treasures Web site, http://oi.uchicago.edu/OI/IRAQ/lh.html.

neither reprinted nor updated. This is regrettable since numerous object photos were supplied by the SBAH only after the booklets were published, leaving many objects unillustrated. As we were painfully reminded in April 2003, facts and figures remain dynamic after a museum looting. Objects thought to be missing turn out to be misplaced or are returned; others are only later noticed to be missing. Paper publications do not provide the flexibility for such frequent changes in a way that computer databases do. Back in 1991, however, access to the Internet was still relatively uncommon, modem speeds were slow, and most computers were ill-equipped to handle graphics files.

Table 1. Web-based resources on the Oriental Institute's home page to the cultural crisis in Iraq following the 2003 war

Oriental Institute Home Page   http://oi.uchicago.edu

Lost Treasures from Iraq   http://oi.uchicago.edu/OI/IRAQ/iraq.html

Iraq Museum Database   http://oi.uchicago.edu/OI/IRAQ/Iraqdatabasehome.htm
• Visualization   An illustrated database of objects from Iraqi museum collections

Preliminary Bibliographies   http://oi.uchicago.edu/OI/DEPT/RA/IraqBibs.html
• Documentation   Preliminary bibliographies of books documenting the contents of the Iraq Museum, the National Library and Archives, and the manuscript collection of the Ministry of Religious Endowments — all in Baghdad — as well as of other damaged or destroyed collections in Baghdad and elsewhere in Iraq

IraqCrisis   https://listhost.uchicago.edu/mailman/listinfo/iraqcrisis
• Communication   A moderated list for communicating substantive information on cultural property damaged, destroyed, or lost from libraries and museums in Iraq during and after the war in April 2003, and on the worldwide response to the crisis

Twelve years, one Iraq war, and one museum looting later, the software to build such a database and the means of making it available via Web browsers are commonly available. From the outset of the database project, time was an essential factor. On April 18, seven days after the museum looting was reported worldwide, we launched Lost Treasures from Iraq (see table 1). A subsidiary site on the Oriental Institute's Web site, it was to become a Web outlet to post news about Iraq's cultural heritage in wartime and to discuss both consequences and possible reactions of the scholarly community in an online forum. Most of the work on the site was split between myself and Charles E. Jones, then Head Librarian at the Oriental Institute Research Archives (now at the Blegen Library, American School of Classical Studies at Athens). As a first step, Jones compiled a comprehensive bibliography on published Iraq Museum registration numbers, which now contains over 12,000 entries. In late April 2003 he launched IraqCrisis, a moderated list devoted to information about Iraq's cultural heritage. As the director of the Diyala Project, the complexities of building an artifact database are quite familiar to me, so the creation of an Iraq Museum database largely fell into my hands, while Karen Terras, a volunteer to the project, did most of the data entry. Setting up a database that publishes potentially stolen objects, displaying images from numerous published and unpublished sources, has legal implications that go far beyond our familiar realms of research and academic publication. Right from the outset, therefore, we decided that our main objectives were to

- aid, not implement, law enforcement
- avoid compromising ongoing investigation
- maintain academic independence
- cooperate on an international level
- incorporate educational components into the Web site
- clearly define target audiences for the Web site

Discussion arose on the types of information that were to be included in our online object database. Five elements we considered to be essential as visual identifiers were (a) photographs or drawings of an object; (b) its material; (c) its dimensions; (d) a short narrative description of the object's appearance and characteristics; and (e) museum and/or excavation find numbers (these number are usually written on the object itself and therefore part of its unique physical characteristics). But what about an object's archaeological provenance or date? Neither element helps in a visual identification, and giving its date might even increase its value on the market. Sophisticated dealers, however, tend to have good reference libraries themselves and those willing to trade illicit antiquities would hardly need our Web site to obtain such information. If, on the other hand, we were serious about reaching the public by integrating educational components into the layout of our site, then date and provenance had to be part of an object's description. Every archaeologist who has ever given a tour through an archaeological site or exhibit knows about the public's fascination with how "old" things are. Archaeological provenance may not exude the same fascination to the public, but it is the scholar's most basic and valuable tool in establishing an object's date, its function within a systemic context, and ultimately, its authenticity. Adding this information also allowed us to highlight why objects recovered in controlled excavations have a much higher scientific value to us than those from the antiquities market, giving us a chance to rationalize our vehement opposition to clandestine excavations and illegal antiquities trade before the public. These latter arguments prevailed in the end, so both date and provenance were included in our database.

- **NON-CONTROVERSIAL**   *Physical Characteristics (essential for object recovery)*
    - photograph(s) and/or drawing(s)
    - material (for example, "stone (calcite)"; "clay (unbaked)"
    - dimensions (for example, "height: x cm; diameter: y cm")
    - narrative description
    - museum number and/or excavation number

- **SOMEWHAT CONTROVERSIAL**   *External data (educational, non-essential for object recovery)*
    - archaeological provenance (site, findspot)
    - date of object

- **HIGHLY CONTROVERSIAL**   Legal status of object
    - current status of object (for example, "stolen"; "returned"; "damaged")

The most controversial listing in our database, however, remained an object's current "status." Various concerns had to be addressed here. To the present day we still do not know how many objects from the Iraq Museum are actually missing. Press reports released in April 2003, which suggested a total loss of the museum's collection (some 170,000 registered objects), fortunately turned out to be false.[11]

Reports published in May and June 2003, putting the total number of missing objects between twenty-five and thirty-nine, however, were equally, if not more, misleading.[12] By September 2003 Colonel Matthew Bogdanos, a U.S. investigator who had conducted an on-site investigation into the museum looting between May and August 2003, had tallied up a figure of some 12,000–14,000 missing objects.[13] Though objects continued to be returned, Donny George, then Director of the Iraq Museum, raised the figure of objects still missing to 15,000 by March 2004, a number that more or less has stayed the same since then (see also George, this volume).[14] These discrepancies created a lot of confusion in the public and for a while undermined the credibility of those scholars involved in the recovery efforts, including ours. The true number of lost objects, however, will only be known after a physical inventory of the museum is completed. Pulling every artifact off the shelf and out of its storage container, however, is time-consuming. A full physical inventory of our own Oriental Institute museum collection, for example, where all objects are in known locations on their shelves and the museum records are readily available, would take years. Now imagine doing this in the Iraq Museum with its ransacked storerooms, objects thrown off their shelves, using a partially destroyed museum catalog, and with an overall lack of security in Baghdad. By 2006, when the worsening security situation in Baghdad had forced several museum employees to leave Iraq, the doors of the museum's storage rooms were welded shut. We therefore should not see a lack of initiative in the absence of a final tally for lost items, and some nasty surprises may still lie ahead, as the fate of the Iraq Museum's cylinder seal collection shows us (fig. 2). Generally thought to be the most comprehensive collection of Mesopotamian seals from excavated contexts

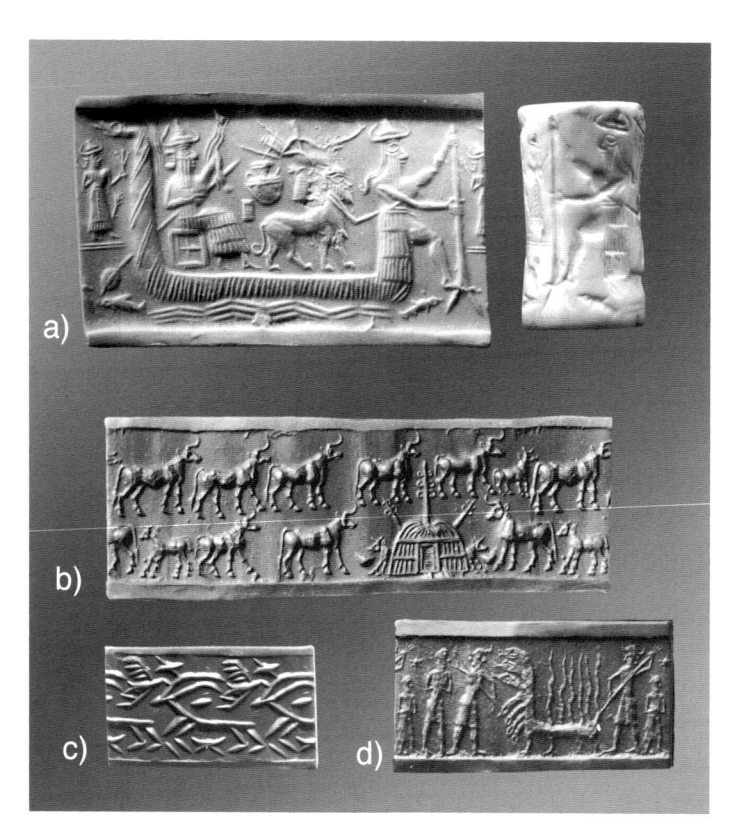

Figure 2. *a)* Cylinder seal from Tell Asmar (ca. 2200 BC) with modern impression of its design (Oriental Institute Museum); *b-d)* modern impression of cylinder seals in the Iraq Museum, *b)* from Khafaje, (ca. 3000 BC); *c)* from Tell Asmar (ca. 2800 BC); *d)* from Tell Asmar (ca. 2200 BC)

---

[11] Some of the early press reports dating between April 12th and 14th that indicated a more or less total loss of the museum's collection include Blair 2003, Hansen 2003, Hendawi 2003, Manier 2003, and Wiltenburg and Schmucker 2003. Note that by April 17, many news outlets already indicated that the losses may have been less severe than reported at first; see, for example, Schofield and Youssef 2003.

[12] The figure 170,000 is the estimated total number of registered objects in the Iraq Museum. Note that many of these numbers can refer to more than one object (e.g., to a box with dozens or even hundreds of beads). Economic constrains since the 1991 Gulf War, resulting in understaffing at the museum's registry, has also slowed down the registration of objects from more recent excavations, meaning that the real number of objects in the museum is much higher.

[12] See, for example, Meier 2003 or Spolar 2003 for these misleading figures. The less than forty missing objects referred to in these reports were objects confirmed to be missing from the museum's public galleries, not including the thousands of objects that were already known at that time to have been stolen from the museum's storage rooms.

[13] Detailed figures are provided by Bogdanos in his report on the museum looting to the U.S. Department of Defense (http://www.defenselink.mil/news/Sep2003/d20030922fr.pdf) and in a briefing on September 10, 2003 (http://www.defenselink.mil/transcripts/2003/tr20030910-0660.html).

[14] Figure quoted by Donny George in an interview on March 4, 2004, with the Jordanian news agency PETRA (http://www.swissinfo.org/sde/Swissinfo.html?siteSect=203&sid=4825280&ticker=true).

worldwide, it initially had been declared safe, since it had been locked away within drawers in one of the museum's storage rooms. It was only when these drawers were finally checked on June 12, 2003, two months after the looting, that it was revealed that a large part of it — 4,875 seals — had been stolen.[15] Seals are among the most treasured collectors' items, and chances of recovering a major part of this collection are slim at best.

In short, even after more than a year we still do not know, with few exceptions, which objects are missing and which ones have been accounted for. By the time a final list is available, however, it will be pointless to publish them in a database — many items will have disappeared for good in illicit collections. Since there was no point in waiting for this list, we decided to define the content of our database as *Objects known to be property of any of Iraq's museums*.[16] While the presence of an object in our database does not necessarily mean that it was stolen, law enforcement should be contacted

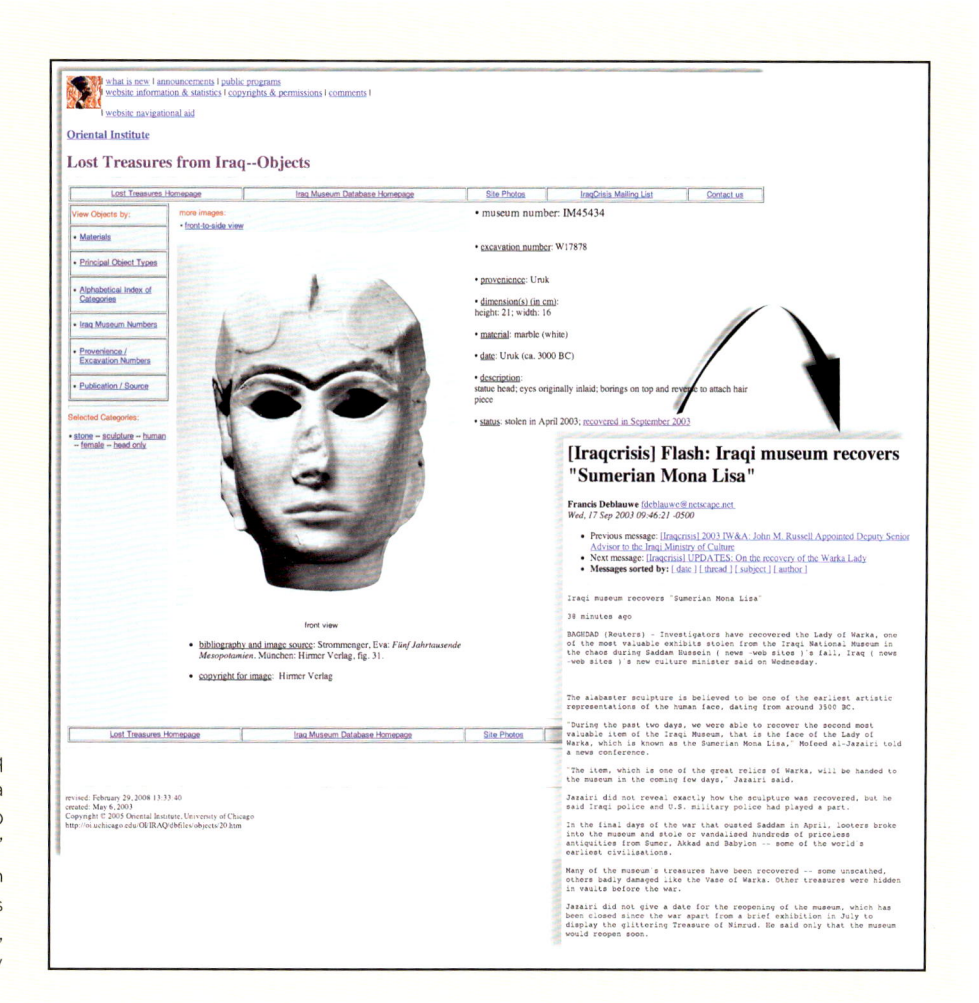

Figure 3. Entry example in Iraq Museum Database: the "Warka Head" (from Uruk, ca. 3000 BC); a hyperlink in the "status" field connects to information concerning the retrieval of this artifact posted on IraqCrisis, displayed in a separate window

---

[15] An initial report dating to June 12, 2003, on the loss of the Iraq Museum seals is posted at IraqCrisis, with a comprehensive update dating to October 10, 2003. (https://listhost.uchicago.edu/pipermail/iraqcrisis/2003-October/000410.html). For an excellent journalistic summary on the implication of the loss of these seals, see Charlé 2003.

[16] While we are clearly focused on the looting of the Iraq Museum in Baghdad, it is necessary to remember that other archaeological museums in Iraq have also been looted, such as the museum in Mosul mentioned above. The museum in the southern city of Nasiriya was reportedly looted as late as May 2004 (https://listhost.uchicago.edu/pipermail/iraqcrisis/2004-June/00025.html).

immediately if any of them should be encountered outside Iraq. A "status marker" in the database indicates if an object is known to be missing, damaged, or has been recovered, the default entry being "unknown." Eventually, our list of objects will be far longer than the actual list of stolen items, but we felt that our resources are used better by adding more objects and information than by constantly re-evaluating if an item in our database should still be listed in it. Should an object be retrieved, it will be annotated in the "status" field. The entry for the "Warka Head" (fig. 3), for example, one of the most famous objects from the Iraq Museum, relates that it was stolen in April 2003 but retrieved in October 2003.[17] A hyperlink to an archived message on IraqCrisis provides further details concerning the recovery of the sculpture.

Unlike the Diyala database, this database was never intended to be a final publication in any sense. Most of the included material had been published in print elsewhere, so an exhaustive repetition of details seemed unnecessary. More significantly, we only have the publication rights for our own material. While we obtained permission from respective copyright holders for every photograph on our site for which we do not hold the copyright ourselves, we neither intended nor sought permission to republish all data pertaining to these objects online. Seeing collections of archaeological artifacts published online is highly desirable, but this has to be the responsibility of the archaeological mission or museum holding the primary data and should not be attempted by outsiders like us. In addition to the copyright holder for images, our database also provides full bibliographic citations for primary publication sources of images. Many of these books are expensive, published in foreign languages, some are out of print, and generally hard to come by. Should an object from the antiquities market with no museum number actually be identified with help from our database, it will not suffice in court to point to our site to prove that this is a "stolen" object. To prove the ownership of this object in a contested case, a prosecutor may have look to a source book or catalog that lists the object as part of the Iraq Museum collection or to produce an eyewitness who can testify that he saw, studied, or photographed the object in the Iraq Museum. To facilitate his work we decided to post the necessary bibliographic data along with each object.

Object categorization within the Lost Treasures of Iraq database requires some explanation (fig. 4). For a non-academic audience it had to be simple, descriptive, and easily understandable. This is where a scholar, who usually categorizes objects in functional or interpretive terms instead of descriptive terms, will run into trouble, no

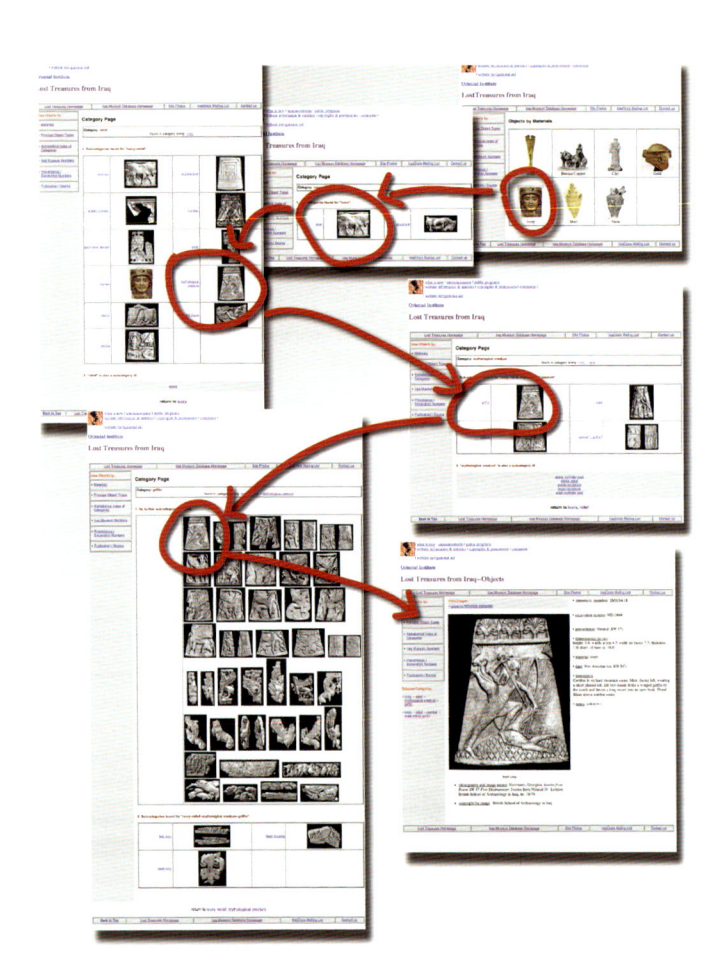

Figure 4. Iraq Museum Database site navigation: starting from a "material overview" page, this examples shows how the ivory object displayed in figure 6 could be located in the database using both narrative and visual clues

---

[17] The URL for the entry on the Warka mask is http://oi.uchicago.edu/OI/IRAQ/dbfiles/objects/20.htm.

matter how hard one tries to avoid pitfalls. Take the term "cylinder seal," for example (fig. 2). Part of it is descriptive since the object itself is cylindrical in shape, but the "seal" component is fully interpretive. While a scholar of the ancient Near East recognizes this object as a tool used in Mesopotamia for bureaucratic procedures, a casual viewer will see a cylindrical stone object with a carved scene. Its identification as a "seal" is based on external, "scholarly" information. Similar pitfalls exist for many other terms used for Mesopotamian artifacts, such as "cuneiform text," "bulla," "votive plaque," "mace-head," "boundary stone," none of which give a lay person any clear concept of what to expect visually. Even if categories are clearly defined, ambiguities remain since different people classify objects differently. Most people, for example, call the famous Warka vase, stolen last April and returned to the museum in pieces last June, a "stone vessel" (fig. 5). While the fact that it is made of stone (alabaster) is unambiguous upon physical inspection of the object, it is not necessarily apparent from a photograph. Its light, yellowish-buff color in photographs may suggest to some people that it is made of clay. The fact that it has four bands of relief decoration is unambiguous even in photographs. If a fragment of its rim actually had gone astray onto the antiquities market, it could be classified as a "relief fragment" without recognizing its being part of a stone vessel. Without such a classification, however, it would not show up in searches for stone vessels and might therefore be missed. In short, many objects have to be added to more than one category.

Figure 5. Left: full view of the Warka vase as restored and on display in the Iraq Museum before April 2003; Right: close-up of top register showing ancient repair. A small fragment of such a vessel, if retrieved on the antiquities market, could be classified as a "relief," missing the association with a vessel, hence the need for multiple classifications for an object in a database. Photo courtesy of Hirmer Verlag

Figure 6. Ivory panel with scenes of one man killing a lion, another man killing a griffin. Neo-Assyrian (ca. 800 BC). Iraq Museum, Baghdad. Photo courtesy of the British School of Archaeology in Iraq

How much — or little — have we achieved during the past five years? That depends on the view one takes.[18] At present, we have posted 1,352 items in the online version of our database. This number may sound impressive, but pales in light of 170,000 registered objects in the Iraq Museum and 15,000 stolen objects. More to the point, by and large we still do not know what is missing and what is not, so the status of most items posted remains "unknown." Cylinder seals, votive statues, and ivory reliefs form the largest corpus of material posted on our site. Most of these items are from Oriental Institute expeditions, and the reasons for that go way past easy access to their data. We already know that many of them are among the stolen items. Some 15 percent of the stolen cylinder seals (over 600 seals) were excavated by the Diyala Expedition — a particularly painful loss since the Diyala seals represent the largest excavated corpus of seals from good stratigraphic context. Currently, we have images and descriptions of 626 seals, including seals from Nippur and Abu Salabikh. Another large corpus of material, provided to us by the British School of Archaeology,[19] consists of elaborately incised ivory panels that were found during the

---

[18] For initial press reports on the release of Lost Treasures from Iraq, see Duffy 2003, Handwerk 2003, Newbart 2003, and Singel 2003.

[19] We are particularly grateful to Georgina Herrmann, who supplied me with the photographs of the Nimrud Ivories; to Stuart Laidlaw (Institute of Archaeology, London) for scanning them; to Nicholas Postgate and Harriet Martin (Cambridge) for sending me photographs and descriptions of the seals and sealings from Abu Salabikh; and to Hirmer Verlag for letting us use images from Strommenger 1962 on our site. Last but by no means least, I want to thank my project volunteers Karen Terras (2003–2006) and Muhammad Abdallah (2007–present) for their tireless and dedicated work.

British excavations at Nimrud, the capital of Assyria during the ninth and eighth centuries BC (fig. 6). The total number of these panels that were allocated to the Iraq Museum is unknown to us, but it must have been in the thousands. Currently we have 485 of them online. Sculpted stone items form the next largest group, of which 156 are currently posted, including the worshipper statues from Tell Asmar and Khafaje (see Hanson, this volume, figs. 2–4).

I cannot say to what degree our Web site has directly helped in the recovery of objects from the Iraq Museum. As long as there are ongoing investigations it is unlikely that we will hear about any results in due course. We have, however, been contacted by representatives of customs and law enforcement agencies from the United States and other countries. If nothing else, our Web site provides numerous examples of what to look out for. Though the educational aspect of our site was conceived as a side product, its impact should not be underestimated. High schools and even colleges have used our site for class assignments. Two years ago, during a visit to Aleppo University in Syria, I was surprised to find students using bound printouts from our Web site as teaching manuals. During assignments at museums or on expeditions these students may well encounter items smuggled to Syria from Iraq, so our Web site may benefit their education in more than one way.

If anything "good" can come of the looting of the Iraq Museum it should be a wake-up call for every museum in the world. Every collection is at risk, not necessarily from warfare or civil unrest, but natural elements such as earthquakes, fire, floods, and inevitable decay due to climatic conditions. Museums should consider what they would do if, for whatever reason, its collection were struck by disaster. This is where museums tend to fall silent. Photographs or drawings cannot replace the actual object, but having some visual record of an object certainly helps to preserve the knowledge of it. There may be a bitter irony in the fact that we are working on a database of objects from the Iraq Museum, a collection half-way around the globe, while our own, intact collection still warrants such a step. Many lessons are learned too slowly and too late — losing an archaeological object physically remains a tragedy, but only if no records of it exist anywhere, it truly loses its significance and meaning for the world of archaeology.

Bibliography

Abrams, Irwin, and Wang Gungwu
    2003   *The Iraq War and Its Consequences: Thoughts of Nobel Peace Laureates and Eminent Scholars.* Singapore: World Scientific Publishing.

Adams, Robert McCormick
    2001   "Iraq's Cultural Heritage: Collateral Damage." *Science* 293, issue 5527 (July 6, 2001): 13. http://www.sciencemag.org/cgi/content/summary/293/5527/13

Atwood, Roger
    2003   "In the North of Iraq Mosul's Museum, Hatra, and Nimrud." *Archaeology Online Features*, June 4, 2003. http://www.archaeology.org/online/features/iraq/mosul.html

Baker, Heather; Roger J. Matthews; and John N. Postgate
    1993   *Lost Heritage: Antiquities Stolen from Iraq's Regional Museums.* Fascicle 2. London: British School of Archaeology in Iraq. http://oi.uchicago.edu/OI/IRAQ/lh2.pdf (screen resolution); http://oi.uchicago.edu/OI/IRAQ/lh2a.pdf (printable resolution)

Blair, David
    2003   "Thieves of Baghdad Rob Museums of Priceless Treasure." *Daily Telegraph*, April 14, 2003. http://www.opinion.telegraph.co.uk/news/main.jhtml?xml=/news/2003/04/14/wmus14.xml

Bogdanos, Matthew
- 2005 *Thieves of Baghdad: One Marine's Passion for Ancient Civilizations and the Journey to Recover the World's Greatest Stolen Treasures*. New York: Bloomsbury.

Charlé, Suzanne
- 2003 "Tiny Treasures Leave Big Void In Looted Iraq." *New York Times*, July 18, 2003. http://query.nytimes.com/gst/abstract.html?res=F20B1FFC38580C7B8DDDAE0894DB404482; reposted at: http://www.michelvanrijn.com/artnews/nytrosen.htm

Deblauwe, Francis
- The Iraq War and Archaeology Blog – News, Background and Comment. Hosted by the University of Vienna. http://iwa.univie.ac.at/

Duffy, Robert W.
- 2003 "Antiquities Experts Post Online Treasures of Baghdad Museum." *St. Louis Post-Dispatch*, April 27, 2003. http://www.centredaily.com/mld/centredaily/news/5783500.htm

Foster, Benjamin R.
- 2003 "Missing in Action: The Iraq Museum and the Human Past." *The Iraq War and Its Consequences: Thoughts of Nobel Peace Laureates and Eminent Scholars*, Irwin Abrams and Wang Gungwu, pp. 295–317. Singapore: World Scientific Publishing.

Fujii, Hideo, and Kazumi Oguchi
- 1996 *Lost Heritage: Antiquities Stolen from Iraq's Regional Museums*. Fascicle 3. Tokyo: Institute for Cultural Studies of Ancient Iraq, Kokushikan University. http://oi.uchicago.edu/OI/IRAQ/lh3.pdf (screen resolution); http://oi.uchicago.edu/OI/IRAQ/lh3a.pdf (printable resolution)

Gibson, McGuire
- 2003a "Fate of Iraqi Archaeology." *Science* 299, Issue 5614 (March 21, 2003): 1848–1849. http://www.sciencemag.org/cgi/content/full/299/5614/1848
- 2003b "From the Prevention Measures to the Fact-finding Mission," *Museum International* 55: 108–18. http://www.blackwell-synergy.com/links/doi/10.1111/j.1350-0775.2003.00446.x/abs/
- 2003c "Iraq National Museum: Interview with McGuire Gibson." By Liane Hansen. *Weekend Edition Sunday*, April 13, 2003. http://www.npr.org/rundowns/segment.php?wfId=1231007

Gibson, McGuire, and Augusta McMahon
- 1992 Lost Heritage 1: *Antiquities Stolen from Iraq's Regional Museums*. Chicago: American Association for Research in Baghdad, 1992. http://oi.uchicago.edu/OI/IRAQ/lh1.pdf (screen resolution); http://oi.uchicago.edu/OI/IRAQ/lh1a.pdf (printable resolution)

Handwerk, Brian
- 2003 "Hunt for Stolen Iraqi Antiquities Moves to Cyberspace." *National Geographic News*, April 29, 2003. http://news.nationalgeographic.com/news/2003/04/0429_030429_iraqlooting.html; reposted at: http://www-news.uchicago.edu/citations/03/030429.oi-ng.html

Harding, Luke
- 2003 "Mosul Descends into Chaos as Even Museum Is Looted." *The Guardian*, April 12, 2003. http://www.ccmep.org/2003_articles/Iraq/041203_mosul_descends_into_chaos_as_eve.htm

Hendawi, Hamza
- 2003 "National Museum, Home to Artifacts Dating Back Thousands of Years, Plundered by Looters." *San Francisco Chronicle*, April 12, 2003. http://sfgate.com/cgi-bin/article.cgi?f=/news/archive/2003/04/12/international1429EDT0591.DTL

Lawler, Andrew
    2001   "Digging In: New Digs Draw Applause and Concern." *Science* 293, Issue 5527 (July 6, 2001): 38–41. http://www.sciencemag.org/cgi/content/full/293/5527/38

    2003   "A Museum Looted: Mayhem in Mesopotamia." *Science* 301, Issue 5633 (August 1, 2003): 582–88. http://www.sciencemag.org/cgi/content/full/301/5633/582

Manier, Jeremy
    2003   "U. of C. Pleads for Iraq Artifacts – Efforts Under Way to Save Treasures." *Chicago Tribune*, April 15, 2003. http://www-news.uchicago.edu/citations/03/030415.gibson-ct.html

Meier, Barry
    2003   "Most Iraqi Treasures Are Said to Be Kept Safe." *New York Times*, May 6, 2003. http://query.nytimes.com/gst/abstract.html?res=F40B11F73B580C758CDDAC0894DB404482; reposted at http://hnn.us/readcomment.php?id=11871

Newbart, Dave
    2003   "Scholars here Make Catalog of Sacked Museum." *Chicago Sun Times*, April 19, 2003. http://www-news.uchicago.edu/citations/03/030419.scholars.html

Polk, Milbry, and Angela Schuster
    2005   *The Looting of the Iraq Museum, Baghdad: The Lost Legacy of Ancient Mesopotamia*. New York: Harry N. Abrams, 2005.

Reichel, Clemens
    2005   "Beyond Cataloguing Losses: The Oriental Institute's Iraq Museum Database Project, University of Chicago." *Visual Resources* 21.1 (March 2005): 93–113.

Renfrew, Colin
    2003   "Reflections on the Looting of the Iraqi National Museum in Baghdad." In *The Iraq War and Its Consequences: Thoughts of Nobel Peace Laureates and Eminent Scholars*, Irwin Abrams and Wang Gungwu, pp. 319–35. Singapore: World Scientific Publishing.

Schofield, Matthew, and Nancy A. Youssef
    2003   "Baghdad Treasures: Museum Raid Looks Planned." *Detroit Free Press*, April 17, 2003.

Singel, Ryan
    2003   "Looted Iraqi Art Displayed Online." *Wired News*, April 28, 2003. http://www.wired.com/news/culture/0,1284,58640,00.html

Spolar, Christine
    2003   "Majority of Antiquities Feared Lost Found at Iraq Museum." *Seattle Times*, May 5, 2003 (originally published in the *Chicago Tribune*). http://archives.seattletimes.nwsource.com/cgi-bin/texis.cgi/web/vortex/display?slug=museum05&date=20030505

Strommenger, Eva
    1962   *Fünf Jahrtausende Mesopotamien*. Munich: Hirmer Verlag.

Watson, Ivan
    2003   "Mosul Museum." *Morning Edition*, May 6, 2003. http://discover.npr.org/features/feature.jhtml?wfId=1253217

Wiltenburg, Mary, and Philip Smucker
    2003   "Looters Plunder in Minutes Iraq's Millennia-old Legacy." *Christian Science Monitor*, April 14, 2003. http://www.csmonitor.com/2003/0414/p08s02-wome.htm

ARCHAEOLOGICAL SITE LOOTING: THE DESTRUCTION OF CULTURAL HERITAGE IN SOUTHERN IRAQ

ELIZABETH C. STONE
STONY BROOK UNIVERSITY

A similar set of circumstances pertain to all areas where archaeological sites are plundered. The first is the presence of a cultural heritage that generates objects of desire to collectors, be they private individuals or museums. Iraq, with its soubriquet "the Cradle of Civilization" clearly fits the bill. The second is a breakdown of local law and order. This happened in Iraq in the aftermath of the first Gulf War, and especially in southern Iraq in the aftermath of the Shiite uprising immediately thereafter. On a visit to southern Iraq in 1992, a colleague and I witnessed the effects of both the burning of government buildings by rebels and the destruction of date orchards as the government tried to restore order. The rumor mill was replete with stories of bandits. The third ingredient behind large-scale archaeological site looting is the poverty of the local inhabitants. The first Gulf War and the Shiite uprising informed Saddam Hussein that his people, and especially the people of the south, hated him. From that time onward, investment in the infrastructure for agriculture in southern Iraq stopped, except for the project to drain the marshes, which itself displaced a large number of people. The

Figure 1. A member of the U.S. Marine Corps investigating recent looting at Larsa, May 2003. Photo by Elizabeth C. Stone

fourth and final ingredient is the opening of international markets for antiquities as a result of an injection of cash by those behind the illegal trade in antiquities. All these factors were in place in Iraq by 1993, and its cultural heritage has paid a terrible toll.

In the aftermath of the first Gulf War the Iraqi State Board of Antiquities and Heritage (SBAH) was starved of funds and its effectiveness and personnel dropped precipitately. But the United Nations Oil-for-Food Programme injected new cash into the department. Some was used to initiate year-round excavations at sites that were worst hit by looting. This was effective in preventing further looting until the archaeologists were recalled to Baghdad in December 2002 as the 2003 war loomed.

After the war, between May 2003 and January 2004, McGuire Gibson, John M. Russell, and the Italian Carabinieri, undertook three helicopter overflights that provided photographic evidence of significant damage to the major sites Isin, Umma, Umm al-Aqarib, Zabalam, Tell Schmid, Bad Tibera, Abbas al-Kurdi, and Mashkan-shapir. Visitors to Adab, Umm el-Hafriyat, Nippur, Larsa (fig. 1), and

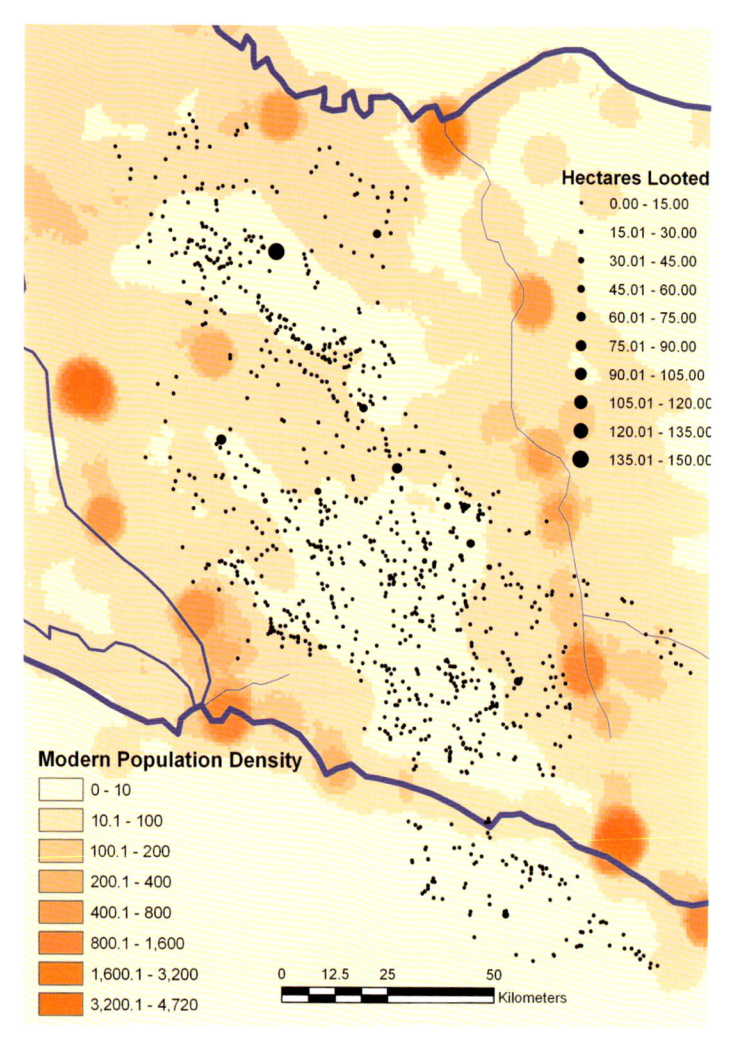

Figure 2. Map showing hectares covered in looting holes for each site in the survey

several other less well-known sites in the Nasiriya area also reported significant damage. These largely anecdotal reports left open key questions regarding the looting: Was the looting restricted to the largest sites, or were sites of all sizes affected? What role does the distribution of the modern population within Iraq play in the damage to sites? Are looters selectively targeting sites dating to particular time periods in search of particular kinds of artifacts? What was the effect of the 2003 invasion and its aftermath on the looting of archaeological sites? The availability of high-resolution commercial satellite imagery taken by the DigitalGlobe Corporation makes it possible to begin to provide answers to these questions, and in the process learn more about the illegal antiquities trade and its workings.

Nearly two thousand sites that were recorded by archaeological surveys[1] in southern Iraq were investigated. Information was cataloged on the dominant date of the surface assemblage, whether the site had been looted, and if so, how badly. Sites where multiple images taken more than a month apart were used to develop an understanding of the chronology of the looting.

---

[1] The results of four archaeological surveys are used in this study: the Eridu and Nippur surveys (Robert McC. Adams, *Heartland of Cities* [Chicago: University of Chicago Press, 1981]; the Uruk survey (Robert McC. Adams and Hans Nissen, *The Uruk Countryside* [Chicago: University of Chicago Press, 1972]; and a recent unpublished survey of Dhi Qar Province conducted by Abdel-Amir Hamdani, the archaeological inspector for that area.

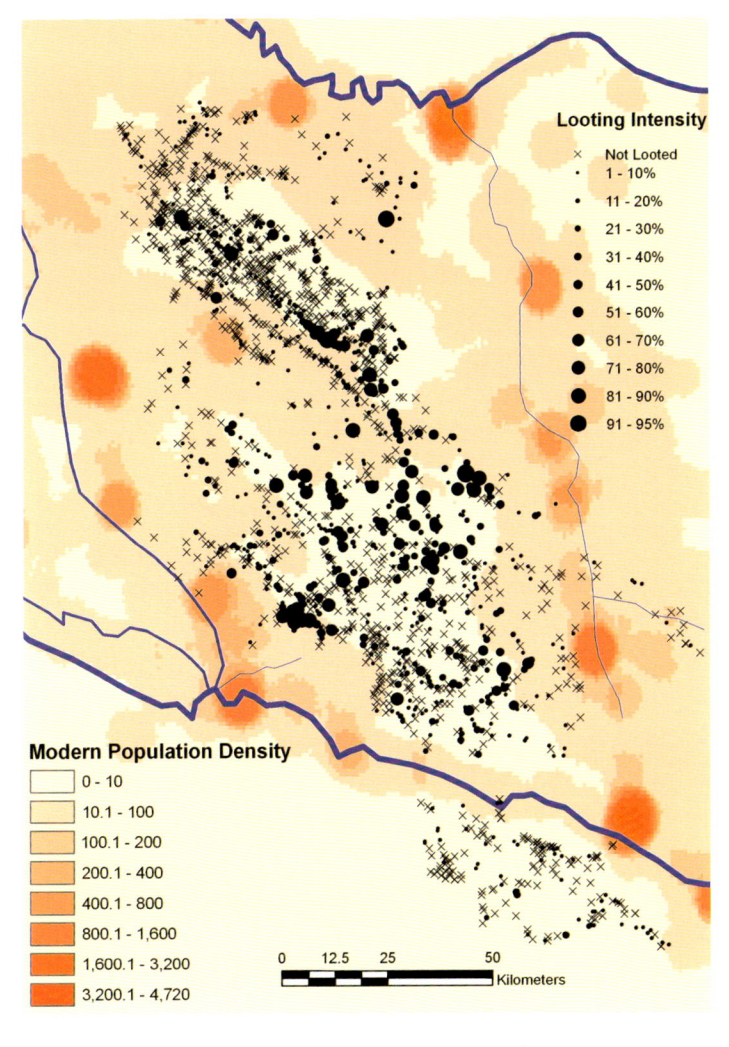

Figure 3. Map showing percentage of each site covered by looting holes

Geography

The sites included in the archaeological surveys — and therefore in our study — were generally located within areas that were desert in the 1960s and 1970s. Agriculture has expanded since that time, with the result that at least some sites that were once in desert are now in cultivated areas. Modern settlement, however, has not shifted as much, and the area under consideration mostly remains thinly settled to this day.

We find the most evidence for site looting in areas that are fairly desertic, but close to irrigated areas with their associated populations (figs. 2–3). The locations of these sites keep them out of the eye of what little security apparatus has existed in Iraq in the past decade, but still close enough to be able to bring in a large work force. However, many looted sites are located deep in the desert areas that mark the borders between provinces. Looting is also very heavily concentrated in the southern part of the Mesopotamian plain, between the modern towns of Nasiriya and Shatra. As one moves north in the direction of Afaq, looting becomes less common, and even farther north, in the area around Babylon and beyond, looting becomes quite rare. This pattern strongly suggests that the motivation for looting comes from the establishment of antiquities markets together, presumably, with mechanisms for exporting the yield. Three towns have been reported to be centers of this trade: Afaq, Rifa'i, and most especially al-Fajr. The latter two are closest to the areas that experience the heaviest looting.

Site Size and Looting

Early helicopter trips focused on large, well-known sites, but a key question motivating this project was to see whether the mass of small and medium-sized sites were also affected. Since very few small sites had been investigated by archaeologists within our study area — and none had been photographed from the air — we were in the dark as to whether these were likely to contain the types of artifacts that would attract looters. The data from the satellite imagery makes it clear that sites of all sizes were targeted (fig. 4). Small and medium-sized sites were equally likely to be looted; some very small sites were almost completely destroyed. We do, however, see an increase in looting in sites larger than 30 hectares — that is, ancient towns and cities. However, the four very large sites, Nippur, Lagash,

Girsu, and Uruk, were generally in better condition. With the exception of Larsa, these larger sites were important enough to have long-term site guards who were effective at preventing looting. This indicates that while the large urban sites, with their palaces and temples, were of especial interest to looters, sites of all sizes generate enough artifacts for their destruction to be worthwhile, even when they are far from population centers.

SITE DATE AND LOOTING

The data collected by archaeological surveys allow us to date the major surface occupation of each site and therefore estimate the types of artifacts likely to be recovered from levels immediately beneath the surface. This permits an evaluation of whether there are specific types of objects that are driving the looting, which in turn indicates the degree to which the demands of outside markets are driving this process (fig. 5).

Not unexpectedly, prehistoric sites dating to the fifth and early fourth millennia BC, which lack the cylinder seals, inscribed tablets, statuary, coins, and other objects that seem to be of interest to collectors, show relatively low levels of looting. This changes in the sites

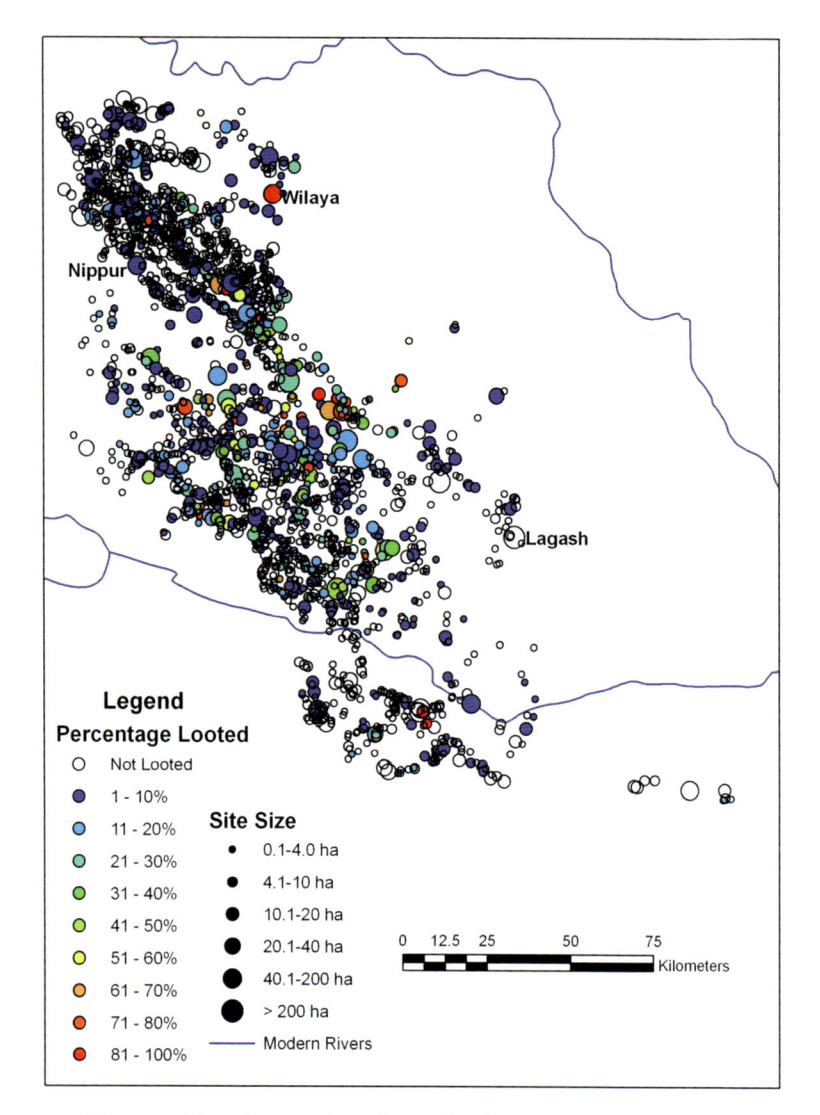

Figure 4. Map showing the relationship between site size and the percentage of the site covered by looting holes

associated with the beginnings of civilization in Mesopotamia, where quite small sites, between 3 and 9 hectares in size, receive the greatest attention. This intensity increases still more at the later Early Dynastic and especially Akkadian sites. All but one of the six sites with Akkadian surface material show evidence of recent looting. The value accorded to Akkadian artifacts is nothing new since many of these sites had already suffered the attention of looters as many as four decades ago. The Mesopotamian art of cylinder-seal carving reached its apogee in Akkadian times, and it must be assumed that it is these objects, then and now, that drive the looting of sites of this period.

Intense looting is also seen at many of the sites dating from late third to second millennium BC (Ur III–Kassite) — especially from sites dating to the earlier part of this time period (through the Old Babylonian period), where attention was focused both on the larger sites and on those less than 9 hectares in size. Although these sites do also yield cylinder seals, these tend to be rather plain, as are the other objects — clay plaques and figurines, jewelry, weights, and the like. But sites of these periods yield the greatest numbers of cuneiform tablets, objects that are to be found — at least in the Isin-Larsa to Old Babylonian periods — not just in public buildings but in private houses as well.

Figure 5. A series of maps examining the pattern of looting based on the date of the dominant surface assemblage at each site. The size of each site, whether or not it was looted, and the percent of the surface covered in looting holes (a measure of looting intensity) for each looted site are illustrated

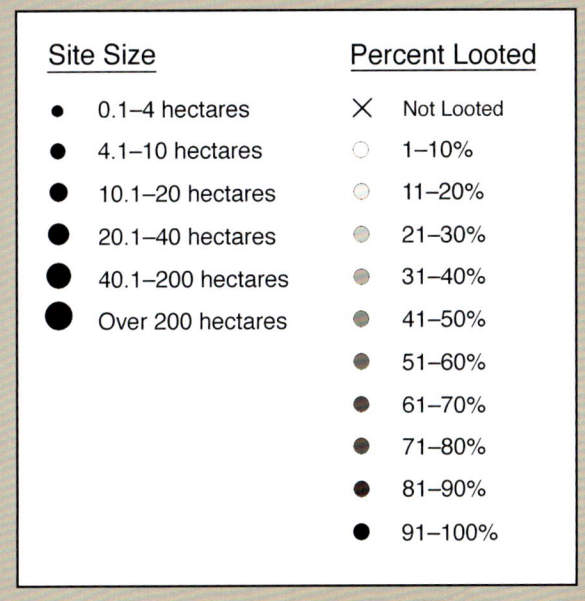

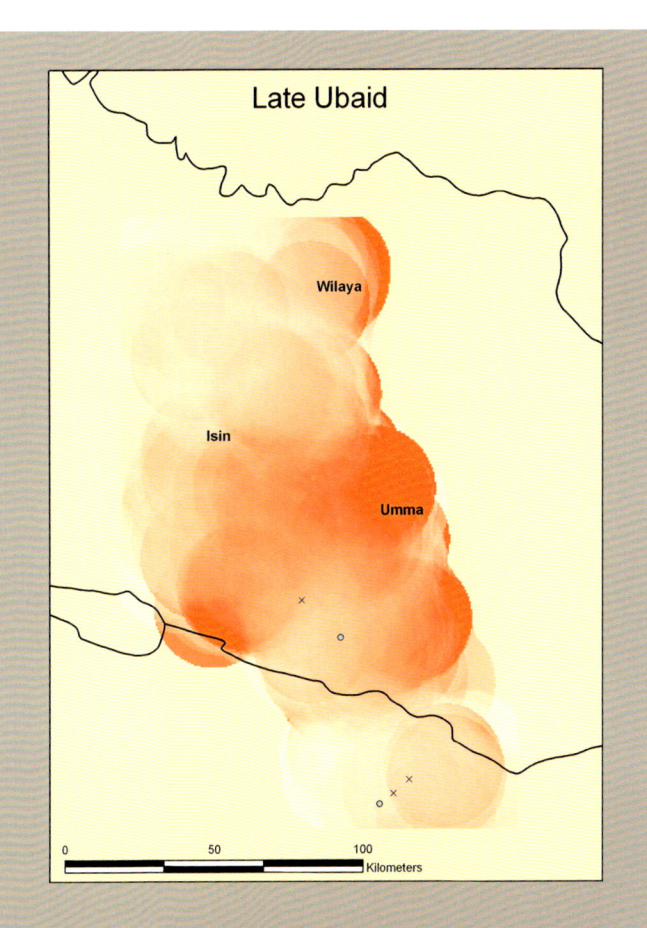

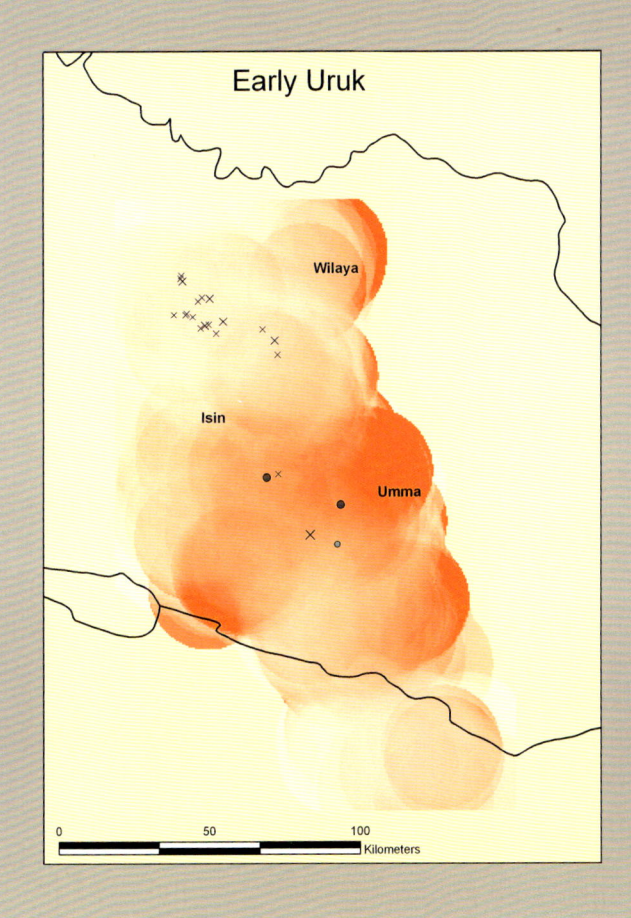

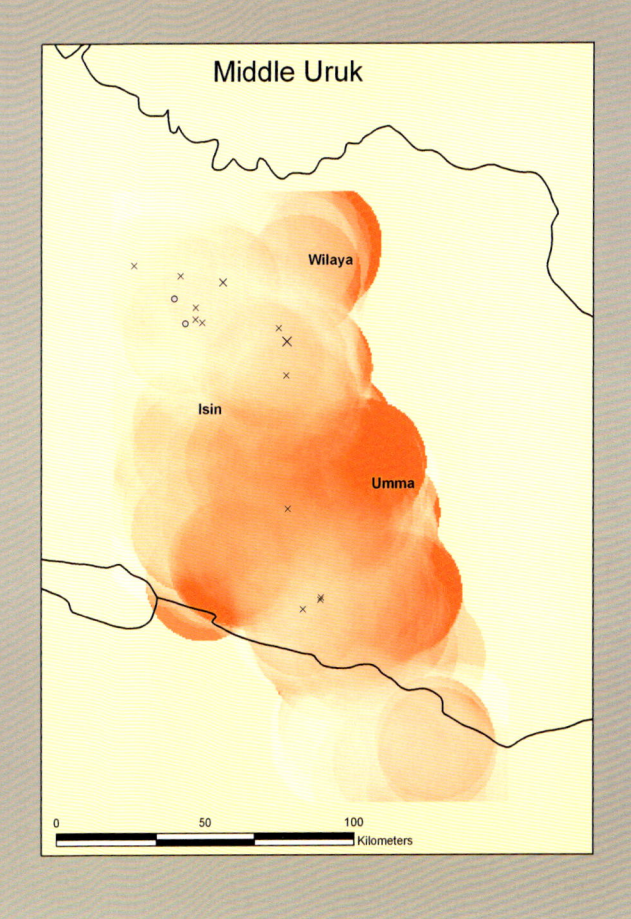

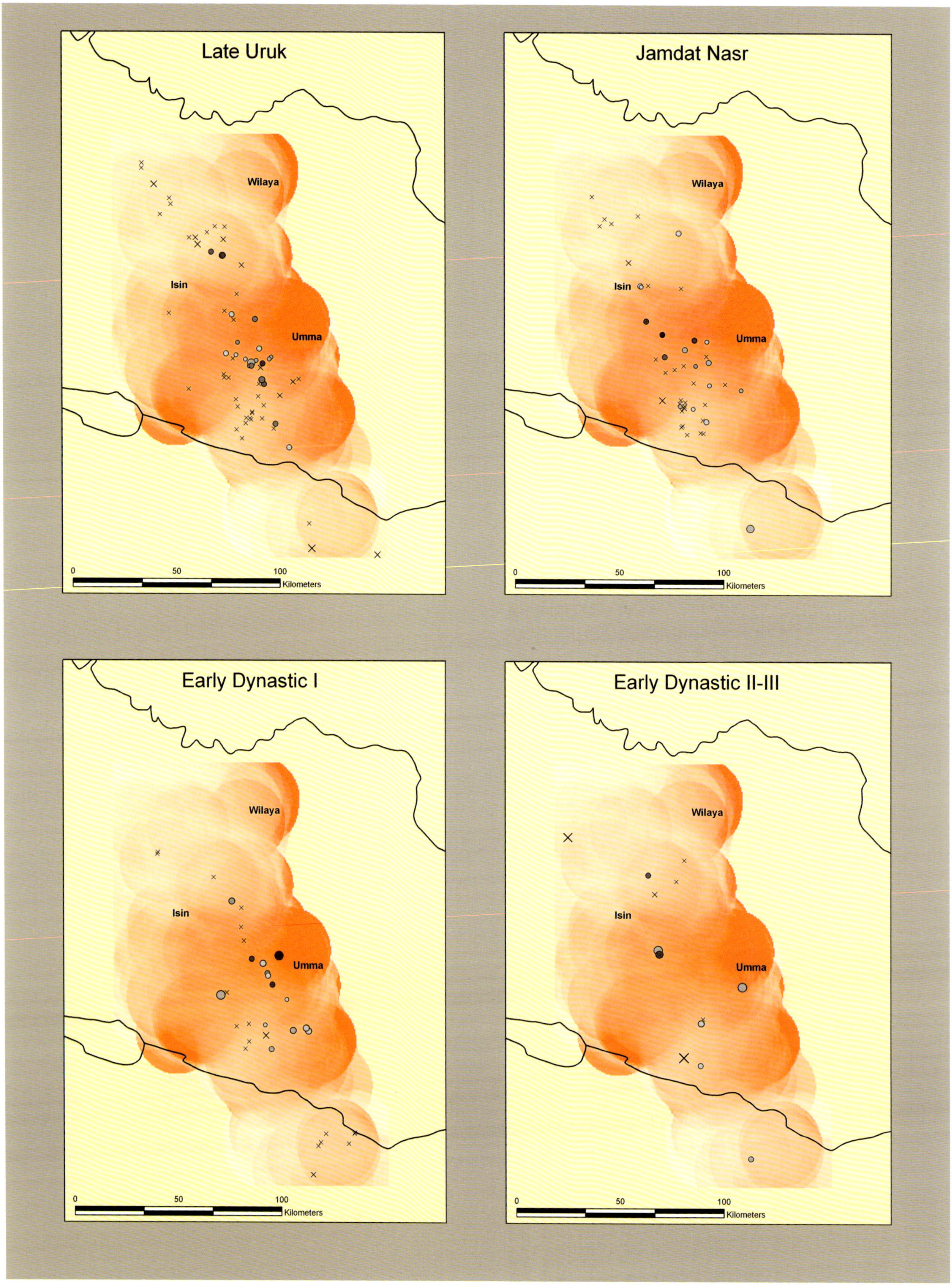
Late Uruk
Wilaya
Isin
Umma
0
50
100
Kilometers
Jamdat Nasr
Wilaya
Isin
Umma
0
50
100
Kilometers
Early Dynastic I
Wilaya
Isin
Umma
0
50
100
Kilometers
Early Dynastic II-III
Wilaya
Isin
Umma
0
50
100
Kilometers

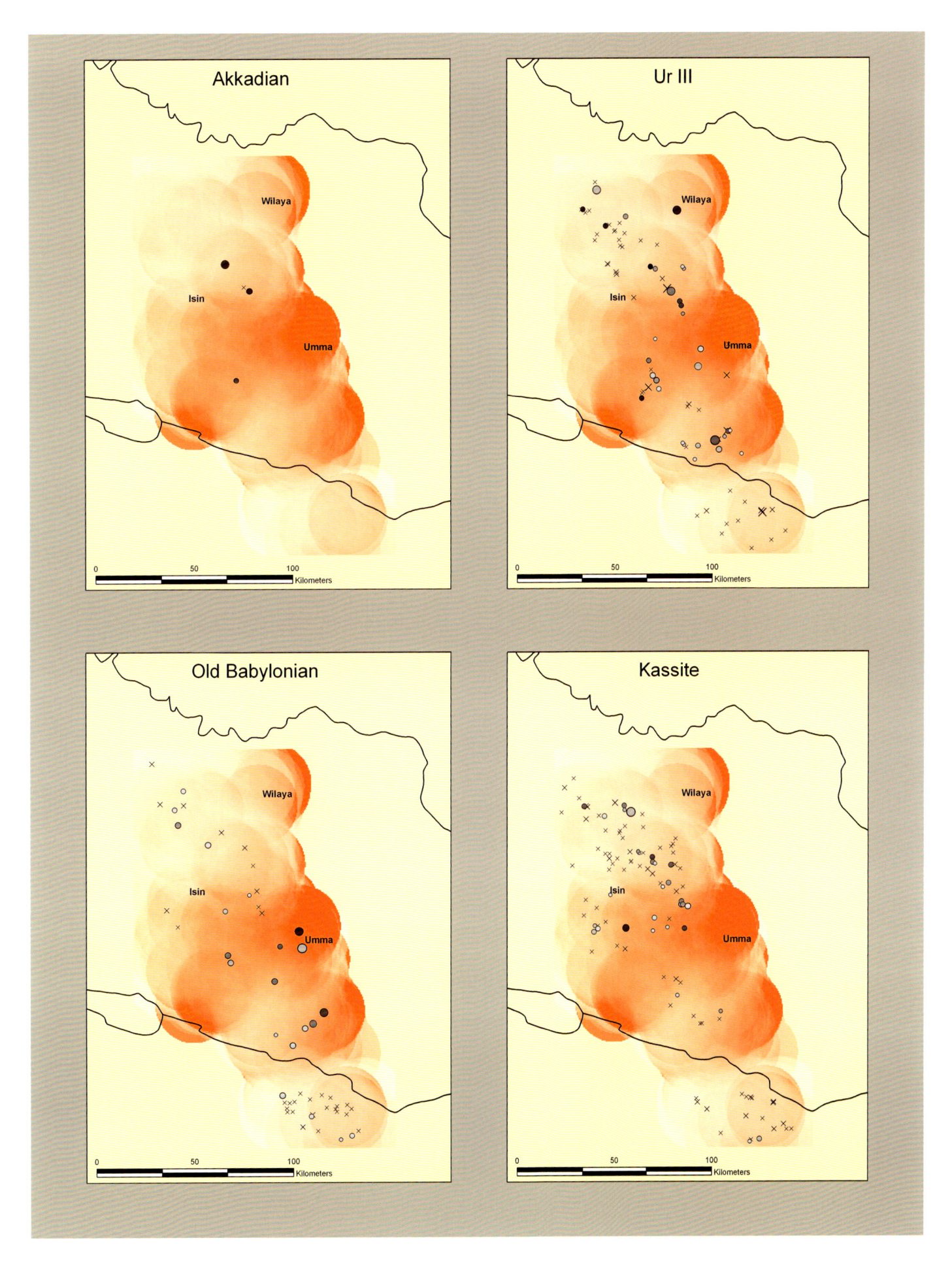

ARCHAEOLOGICAL SITE LOOTING

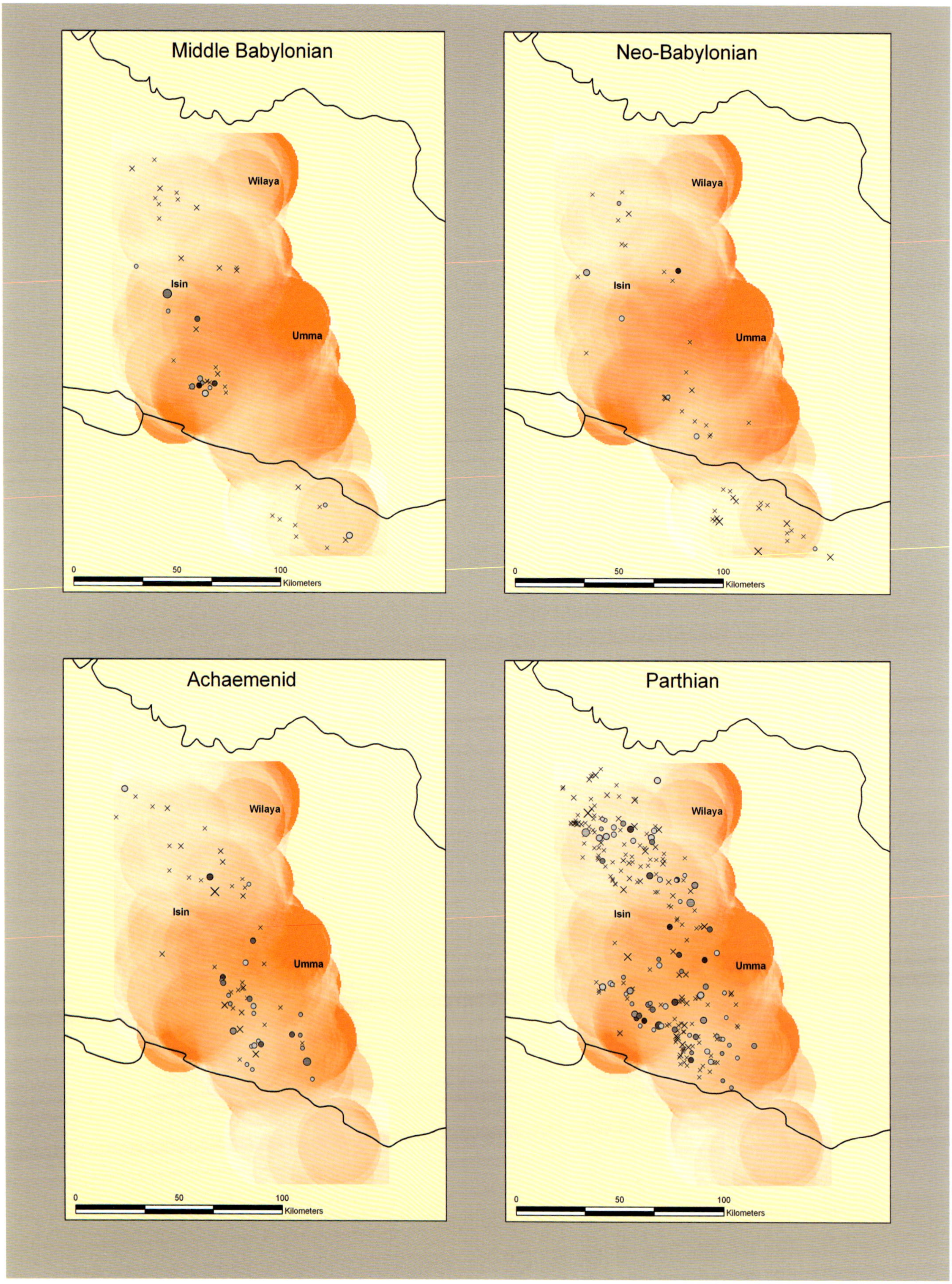
Middle Babylonian
Wilaya
Isin
Umma
0
50
100
Kilometers
Neo-Babylonian
Wilaya
Isin
Umma
0
50
100
Kilometers
Achaemenid
Wilaya
Isin
Umma
0
50
100
Kilometers
Parthian
Wilaya
Isin
Umma
0
50
100
Kilometers

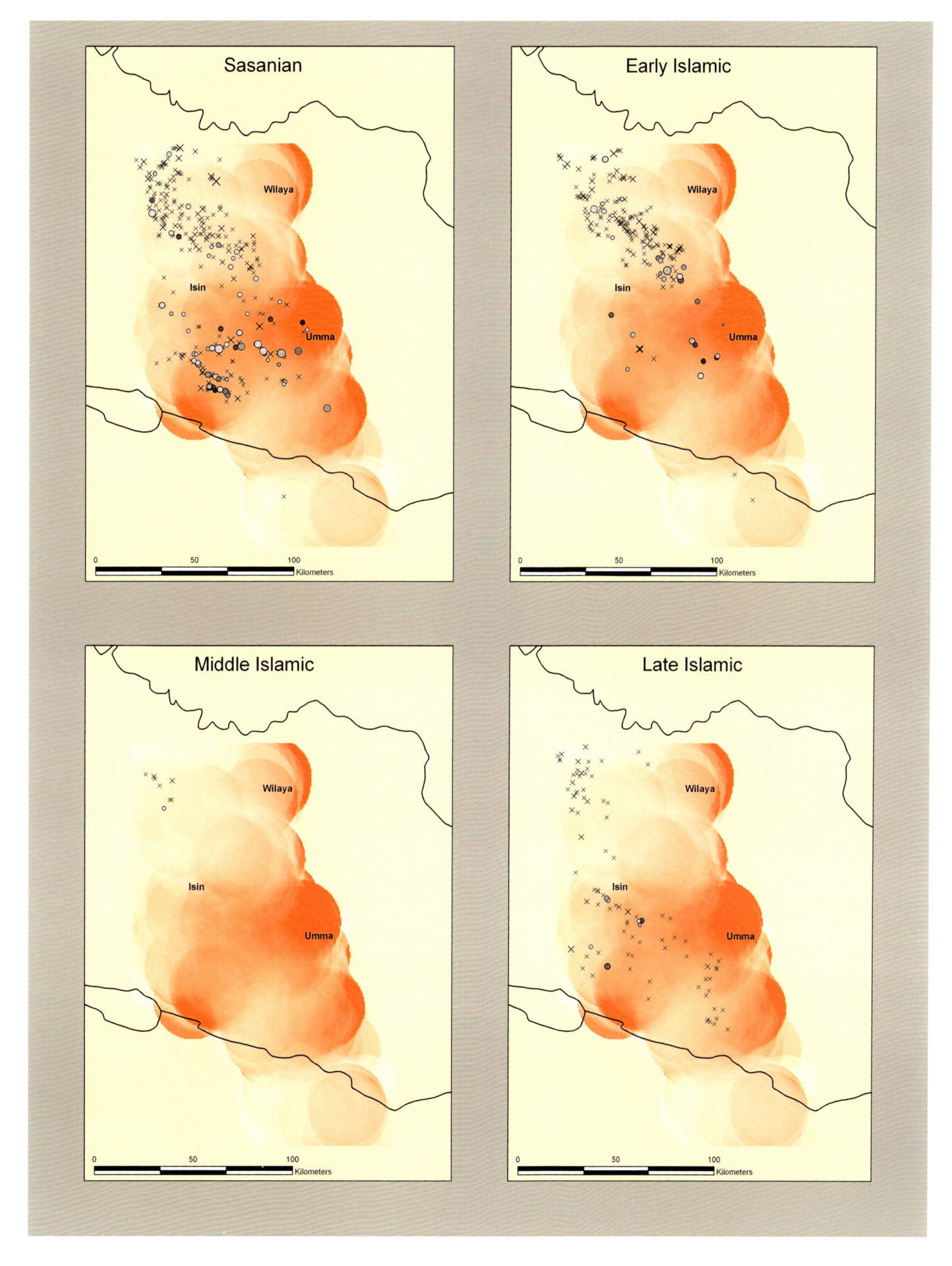

ARCHAEOLOGICAL SITE LOOTING

Sites dating to the Neo-Babylonian period, though common, were left largely intact, perhaps because southern Mesopotamia was something of a political backwater at that time. Achaemenid period sites were also not heavily targeted. Parthian and, to a lesser extent, Sasanian sites, on the other hand, suffered broad-scale damage. The archaeological record from these sites is dominated by early coins and jewelry associated with cemeteries. Although coins continue into later periods, by the Islamic period burials are no longer accompanied by grave goods, perhaps explaining the drop-off in looting of sites of this age.

These data indicate that the date of the surface assemblages of sites does indeed have a profound impact on the likelihood that they will be looted. Sites apt to yield the best cylinder seals (Akkadian), cuneiform tablets (Ur III and Old Babylonian), and early coins (Parthian and Sasanian) show much more evidence for looting than sites of other periods.

The Chronology of Looting

It is possible to track the timing of the looting with the aid of imagery spanning different times. It is also possible to distinguish fresh from older looting, since the sharp edges of fresh looting holes become eroded over time by the action of the wind, which also partially fills them with dust. Approximately one-quarter of looted sites in Iraq are documented with images spanning more than one month, allowing some correlation to be made between the action of the looters and recent political events in Iraq. However, the

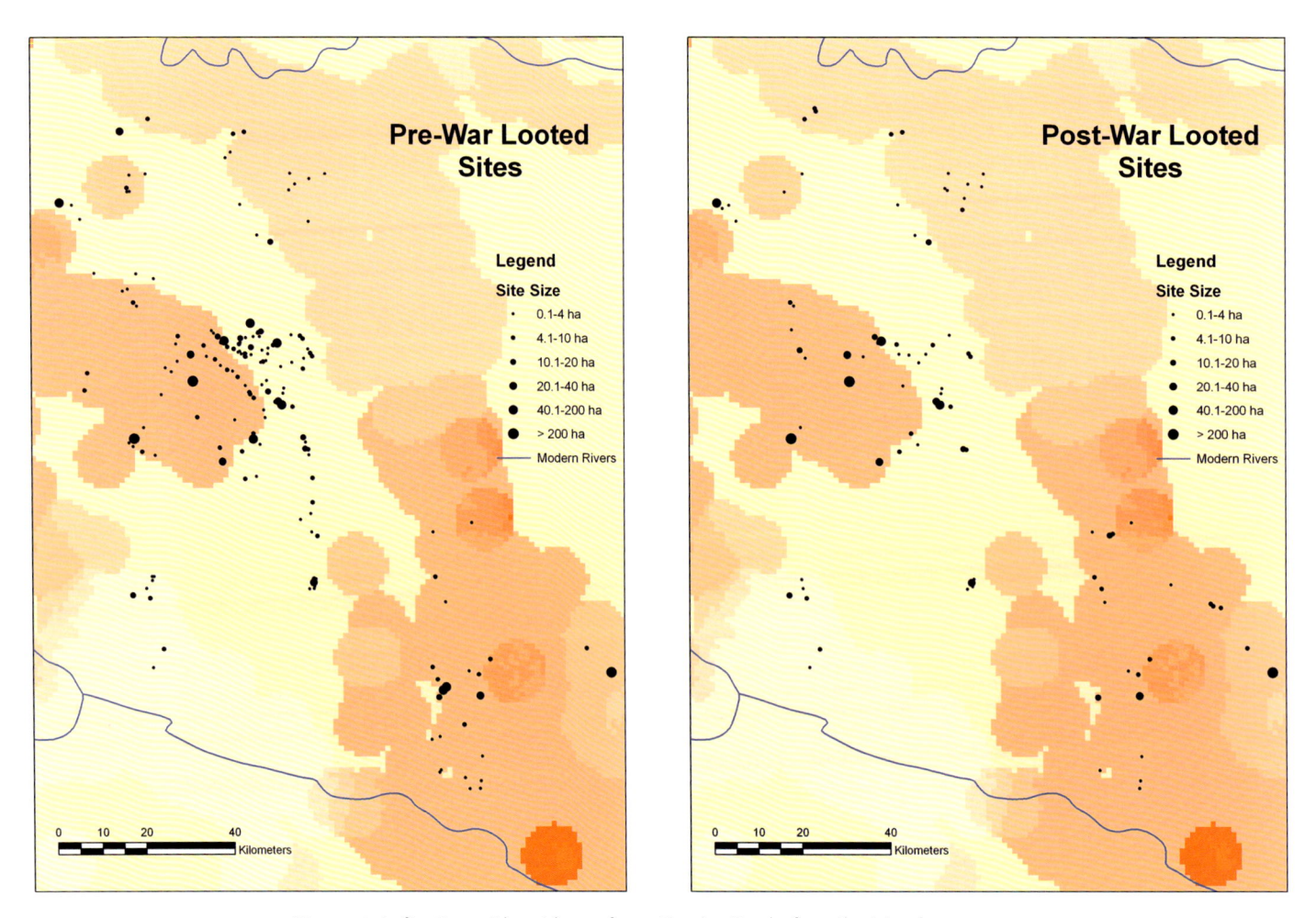

Figure 6. Left, sites with evidence for active looting before the March 2003 war;
right, sites with evidence for active looting following the March 2003 war

majority of the DigitalGlobe imagery available to us was taken either immediately before or after the 2003 war, and only a very small portion of our sample has imagery as late as 2006–2007. Unfortunately, apart from the site of Ur, which is within the confines of the Coalition Air Base at Talil, we have no post-2003 imagery for any major sites and can therefore say little about their current condition.

Our data suggest that the mass of small to medium-sized sites lying unguarded in the countryside were treated differently from the large, well-known sites. The many small and medium-sized sites show evidence of intense looting immediately before the war, suggesting that the threat of hostilities — and presumably the mistaken expectation of increased security thereafter — stimulated an unprecedented level of activity.

In the immediate post-war period, by contrast, most of these sites show little change and the holes that were visible in the earlier imagery have been smoothed by erosion (fig. 6). Although the sample is small, it appears that as the summer of 2003 progressed looting resumed at some of the sites that had been attacked before the war, though at least two-thirds remained untouched. Some sites show evidence for intense looting in the autumn of 2003, but this seems to have died down again later. The rare instances where we have multiple images of looted sites beginning in early 2003 and continuing into 2004–2006 suggest that there was little looting at these smaller sites during the last part of our time sample (fig. 7).

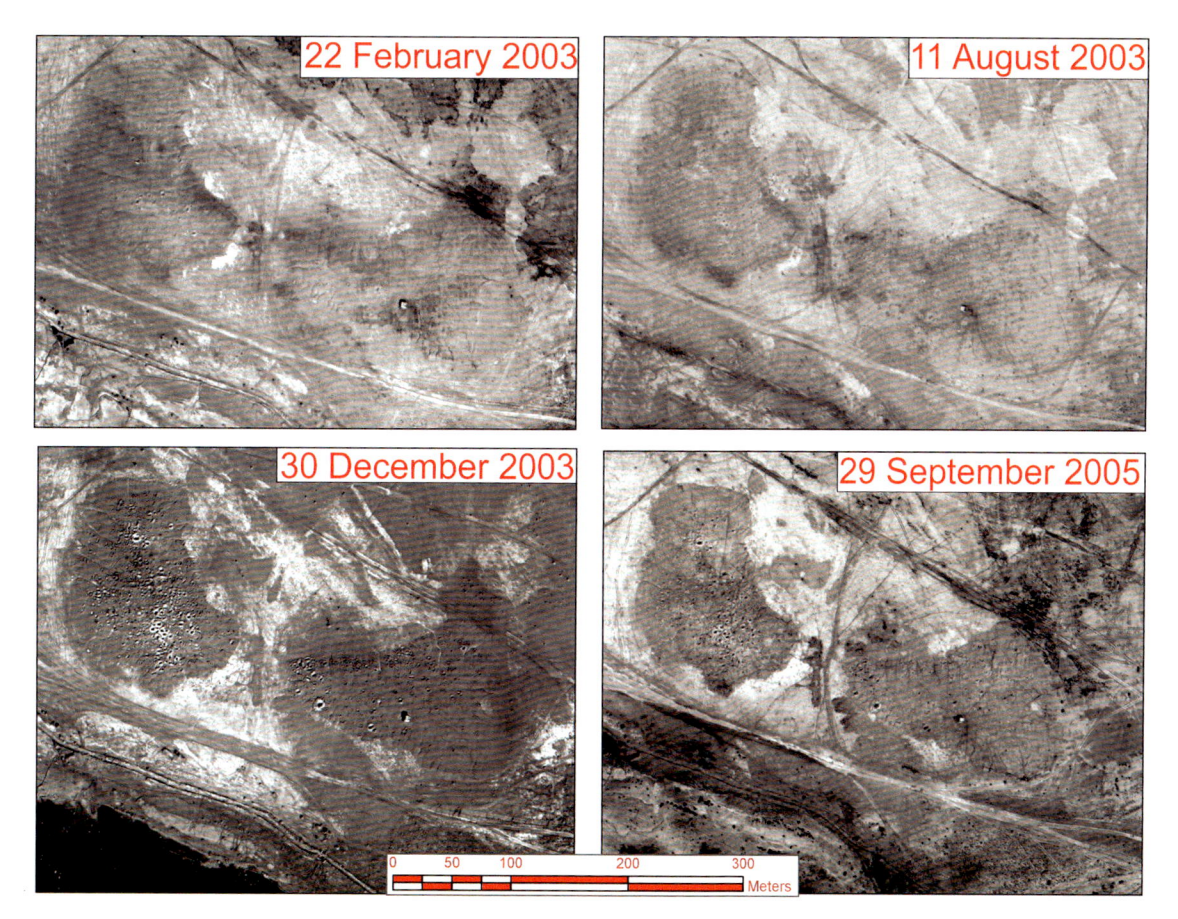

Figure 7. Dhi Qar Survey Site 238. The images from February and December 2003 show evidence of recent looting, whereas those dating to August 2003 and September 2005 do not.
Photo courtesy of DigitalGlobe Corporation

The situation with the larger sites, all of which had site guards (some of whom were more effective than others), is quite different. It is perhaps not surprising that among the major sites excavated by foreign expeditions, Nippur and Uruk have fared best, perhaps because of the long history that local residents have had as excavators employed by foreign archaeological missions. There was only minor damage at Nippur and almost no damage at Uruk. By contrast, Larsa, a site excavated for decades by the French but whose guard had been murdered during the 1991 uprising, was very badly damaged. The eastern half of this ancient city was so badly looted in early 2003 that the SBAH used bulldozers to refill the holes as a means of discouraging further looting, but when a group from *National Geographic* visited the site in May 2003, there was ample evidence of recent looting on the western half of the site (fig. 1). Fortunately, the looters have not had access to earth moving machinery. However, Eridu Site 13, a small, early second-millennium BC site located just to the east of the boundary of the Talil Air Base, was completely flattened between August 2004 and August 2005 as part of the development of the base (fig. 8).

The damage to Isin (fig. 9) has been widely reported. The UNESCO group that made a visit of inspection in June 2003 reported that looters were tunneling down to reach levels dating to the very earliest development of civilization in Mesopotamia. This deep looting can be identified in the DigitalGlobe imagery both by the larger size and blackness of the holes, and by the darker color of the

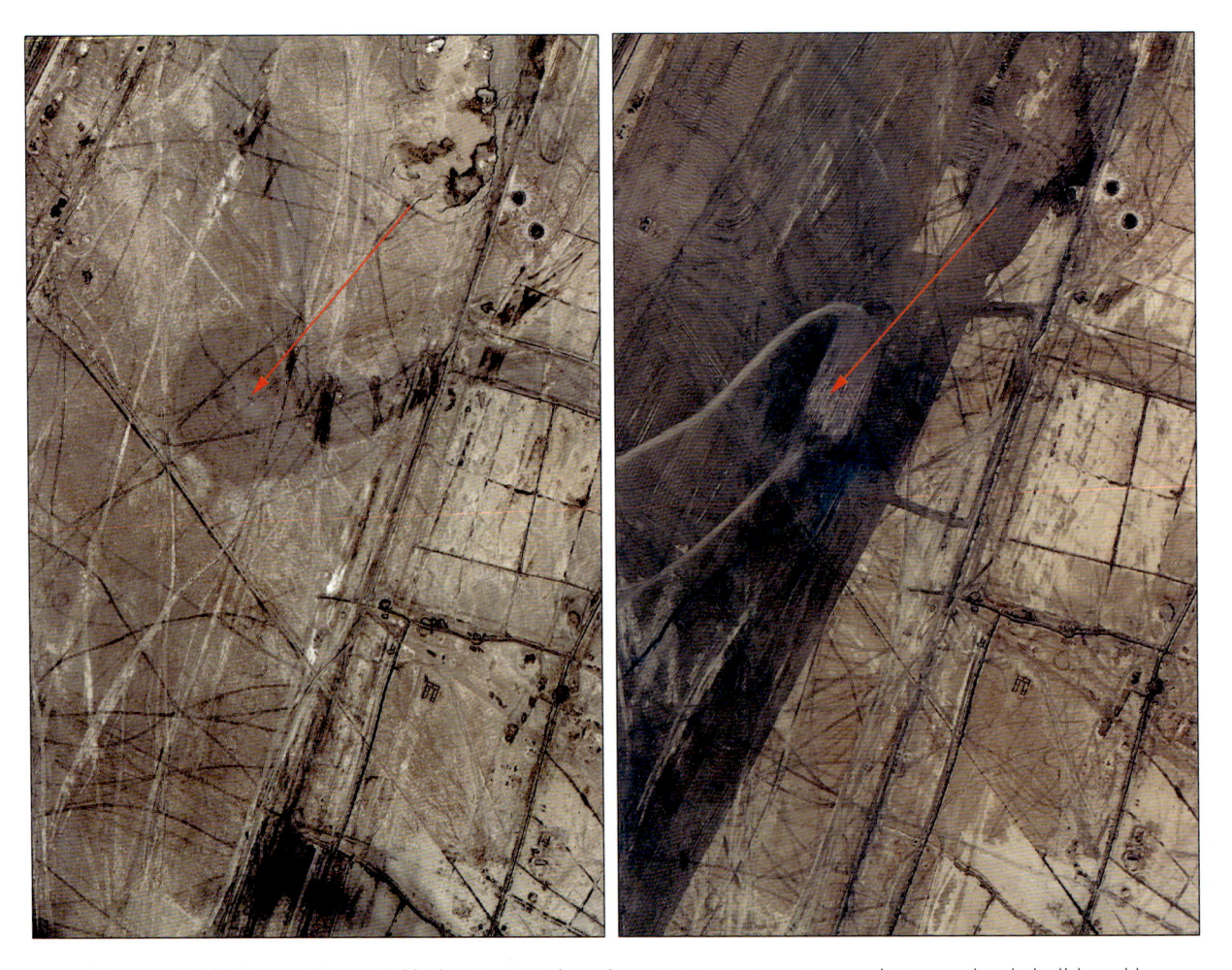

Figure 8. Eridu Survey Site 13, Talil, showing it to have been intact in August 2004 but completely bulldozed by August 2005. Photo courtesy of DigitalGlobe Corporation

ARCHAEOLOGICAL SITE LOOTING

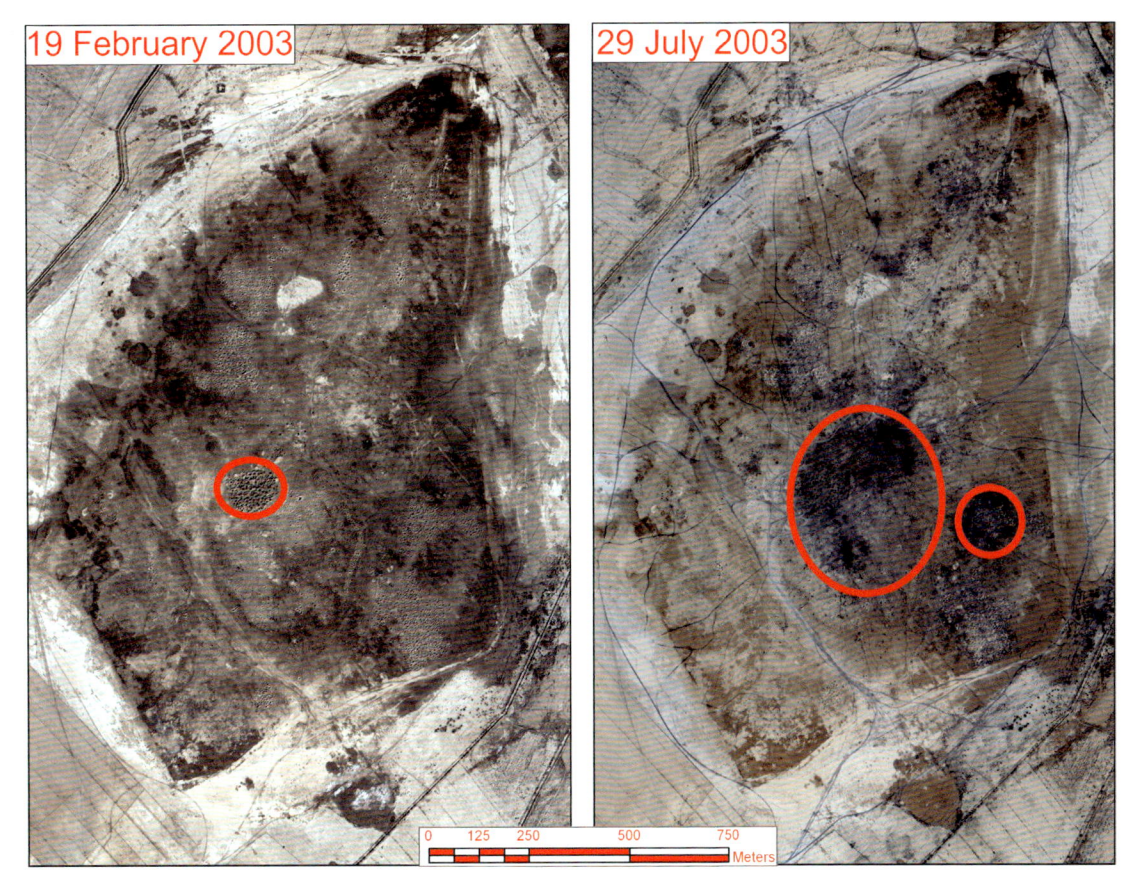

Figure 9. Image shows a small area of deep looting at Isin in February 2003 and much larger areas in July 2003. Photo courtesy of DigitalGlobe Corporation

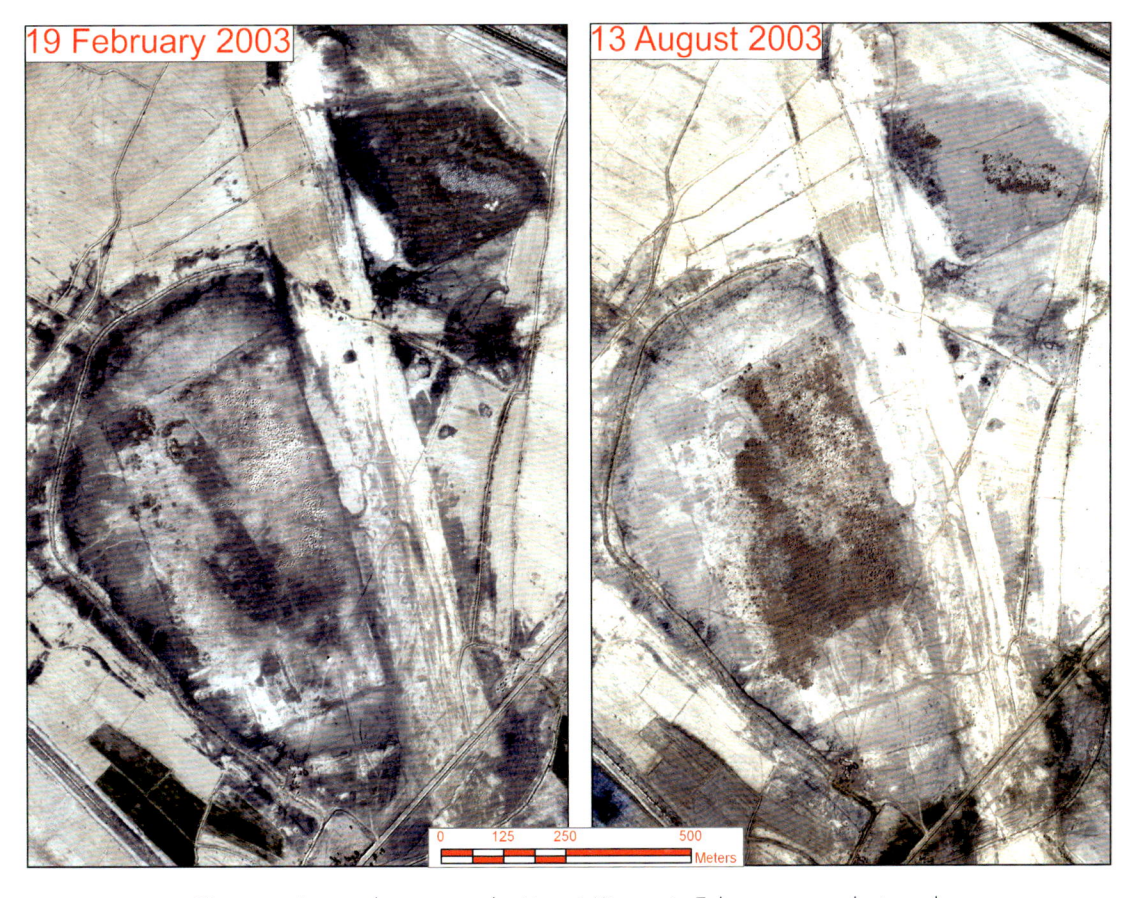

Figure 10. Image shows some looting at Kissura in February 2003, but much more widespread looting by August 2003. Photo courtesy of DigitalGlobe Corporation

77

excavated soil. Isin is the only site where this is evident. The deep looting commenced in February 2003 and accelerated immediately following the war.

As described above, in 1999 the SBAH initiated a program of year-round excavations at some major sites that had experienced severe looting after 1994. When these expeditions were withdrawn late in 2002, the looters returned and inflicted further damage on the important late third- to early second-millennium sites of Tell el-Wilaya, Umma, and Umm al-Aqarib. Zabalam and Tell Schmid had already been very extensively looted before the Iraqi rescue excavations, and subsequent looting has not expanded the area under attack.

Of the major sites that were left largely untended, Bad Tibera was already largely destroyed by the eve of the war, and Kissura, which had suffered one wave of looting before the end of 2000, experienced a second, much more devastating attack between February and August 2003 (fig. 10). Some sites, such as Shuruppak, had suffered only scattered looting before the war, but we have no subsequent imagery and do not know their fate.

Occupation

Looters are not the only ones to damage Iraq's archaeological sites. Occupation forces have also wrought significant damage. The creation of a military camp on Babylon by Coalition forces put severe strain on one of the most important archaeological sites in Iraq. Once again, DigitalGlobe imagery documents what happened and when. These images indicate that one of the more egregious acts, the excavation of large portions of the northeastern corner of Babylon's inner city to provide soil for filling sandbags (fig. 11), happened during the first few months of occupation, when the United States was in charge of the camp. The other most significant damage occurred later, after Polish troops had taken over the camp, and included flattening archaeological areas in order to make parking lots (fig. 12) and the bulldozing of long trenches in the sacred area near the ziggurat (the "Tower of Babel").

Another site occupied by U.S. troops is Ur, which has been included in the occupied zone associated with the nearby Talil Air Base. The most problematic aspects of the Talil base are the recent construction of a new entrance to the base on the ancient suburbs of Ur and the complete destruction by bulldozing between 2004 and 2005 of a 3 hectare site dating to the time of Hammurabi (fig. 8).

It has been argued that the presence of Coalition troops at sites such as Ur and Babylon helps protect them from the attention of looters. But both sites had a large contingent of site guards perfectly capable of fending off looters. Moreover, both were located in areas that had suffered only minor looting of large sites dating to the key time periods lying unprotected in the desert. That Babylon and Ur, two of the most famous of Mesopotamian sites, were not only chosen to be locations for military camps, but once chosen were also treated in this way will remain one of the stains on the occupation of Iraq.

Conclusions

Site looting in Iraq has been pervasive, with sites of all sizes and periods affected. Emphasis, however, has been on those sites dating to periods most likely to generate cylinder seals, cuneiform tablets, and early coins. Although the availability of labor and the seclusion of sites did affect which sites were targeted for intensive looting, more important is the period of occupation, which is directly related to the types of artifacts likely to be found. At present, recent legislation against the import of artifacts from Iraq seems to have closed down the market. Our data suggest that the large amount of material that has been looted but cannot be easily sold has had a dampening effect on looting in Iraq in recent years.

ARCHAEOLOGICAL SITE LOOTING

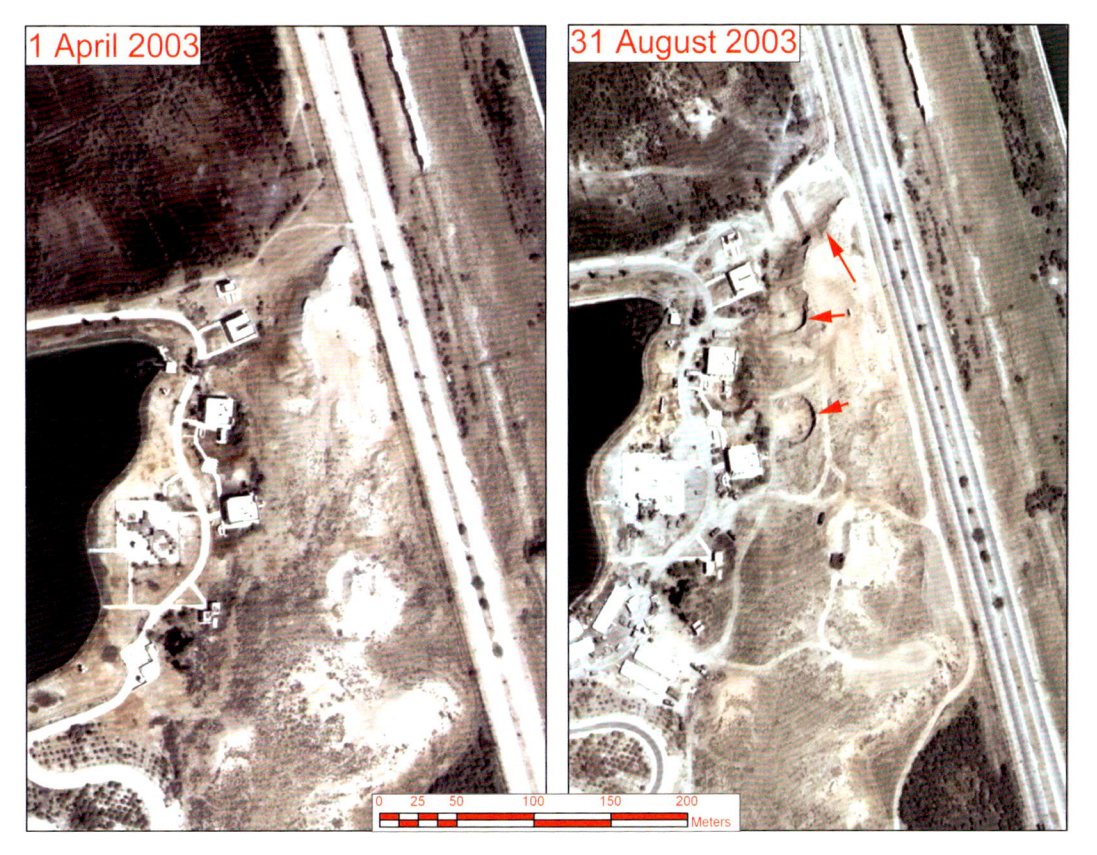

Figure 11. Arrows point to damage caused by excavations for soil to fill sandbags during the American occupation of Babylon. Photo courtesy of DigitalGlobe Corporation

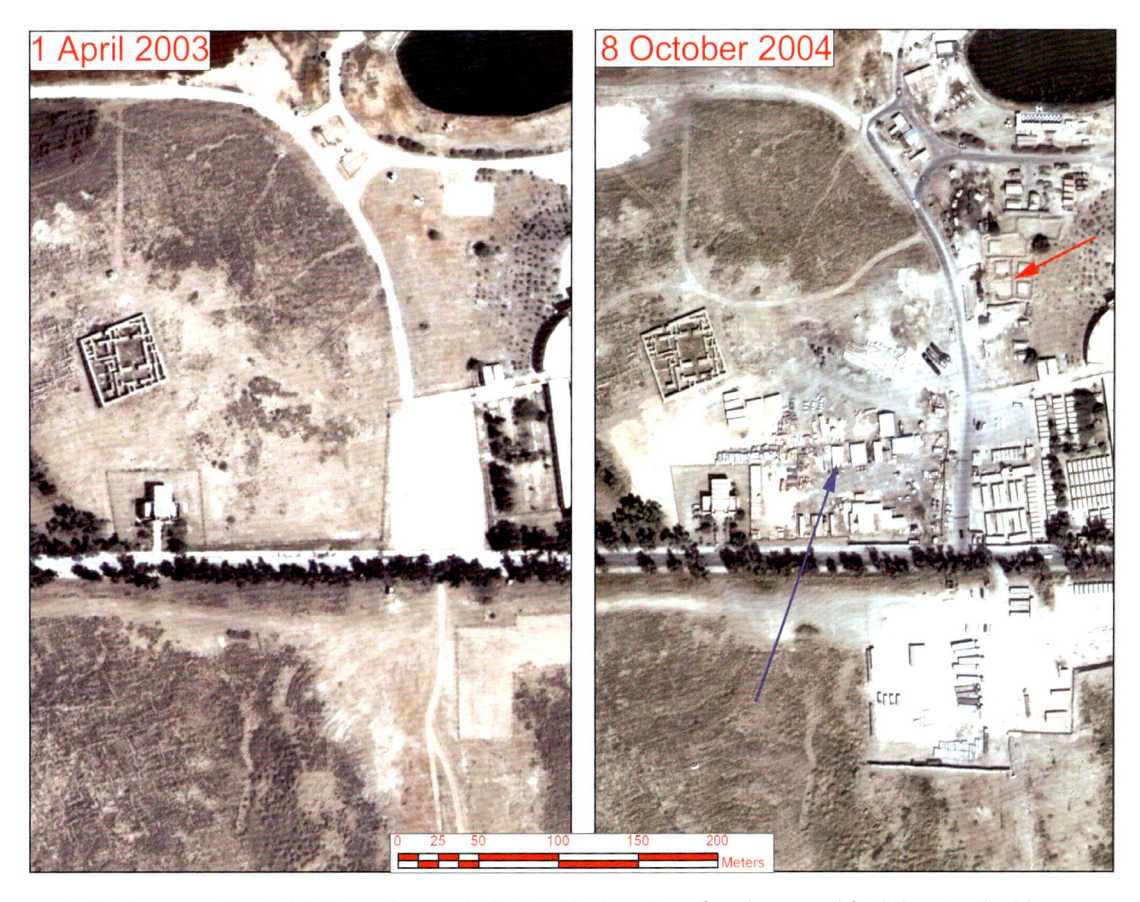

Figure 12. In the image on the right, the red arrow indicates the location of underground fuel depots; the blue arrow points to the flattening of part of the mound to establish a parking lot at Babylon during the American and Polish occupations at Babylon. Photo courtesy of DigitalGlobe Corporation

The imagery we have studied, much of which does not cover periods later than the immediate aftermath of the 2003 war, documents an area of some six square miles of looting holes. This represents an area one hundred times greater than has ever been excavated by archaeologists and the hundreds of thousands, perhaps millions, of tablets and other artifacts recovered by looters seem to have gone underground. In the long term, the destruction of cultural heritage that we have seen in Iraq will only stop if the collectors of cuneiform tablets, coins, cylinder seals, and the like cease their activities. In the short term, we need to support the loyal members of the SBAH who fight the scourge of looting and find ways to recover and preserve the artifacts that have already been ripped out of the ground.

LEGAL ASPECTS OF PROTECTING ARCHAEOLOGICAL HERITAGE IN TIME OF WAR: THE PARADIGM OF IRAQ

PATTY GERSTENBLITH
DEPAUL UNIVERSITY

The legal regime for protecting cultural heritage during armed conflict and for controlling the international market in looted antiquities is an amalgam of international treaties and national laws. The two primary international conventions that address these issues are the 1954 Hague Convention on the Protection of Cultural Property in the Event of Armed Conflict and the 1970 UNESCO Convention on the Means of Prohibiting and Preventing the Illicit Import, Export and Transfer of Ownership of Cultural Property. However, by their nature, international conventions bind only those nations that have become parties to the convention through a formal process such as ratification and, only to the extent that a state party has enacted implementing domestic legislation. Both these factors limited the effectiveness of the legal regime in preventing the looting of sites and cultural institutions in Iraq during the first and second Gulf Wars and in discouraging the subsequent sale of looted artifacts on the international market.

THE 1954 HAGUE CONVENTION

The 1954 Hague Convention is based on earlier international instruments concerning the law of the conduct of warfare, particularly the Lieber Code of 1863 and the 1899 and 1907 Hague Conventions, and was adopted in the wake of the massive cultural looting of World War II. The 1954 Hague Convention consists of three parts: the main convention and its two protocols. The First Protocol was written in 1954, and the Second was written in 1999 in response to the experiences of the Balkan wars. The Second Protocol did not come into effect until 2004 and none of the major parties to the current Iraq conflict have ratified it, so it has not had any impact on the protection of sites in Iraq.

Article 1 of the convention defines "cultural property" as

> movable or immovable property of great importance to the cultural heritage of every people, such as monuments of architecture, art or history, whether religious or secular; archaeological sites; groups of buildings which, as a whole, are of historical or artistic interest; works of art; manuscripts, books and other objects of artistic, historical or archaeological interest; as well as scientific collections and important collections of books or archives...; buildings whose main and effective purpose is to preserve or exhibit the movable cultural property ... such as museums, large libraries and depositories of archives, and refuges intended to shelter, in the event of armed conflict, the movable cultural property....

The two core requirements of the convention are to safeguard and to respect cultural property. The first obligation of parties to the convention is to "prepare in time of peace for the safeguarding of cultural property situated within their own territory" by taking whatever steps they consider appropriate to protect their cultural property from the effects of warfare (Article 3).

During warfare, parties to the convention "undertake to respect cultural property situated within their own territory as well as within the territory" of other parties to the convention (Article 4). This means that during hostilities, nations must refrain from using cultural property as well as the area near any cultural property for strategic or military purposes if this would expose the property to harm during warfare. In addition, parties to the convention must refrain "from any act of hostility directed against such property ... [and] from any act directed by way of reprisals against cultural property." Thus nations that are engaged in military conflict must not target cultural sites and monuments. However, there is a significant exception to this obligation "in cases where military necessity imperatively requires such a waiver." This means that if attacking a cultural site or monument is necessary in order to achieve an imperative military goal, then the military necessity supersedes and the protections of this article are lost. The convention also requires a party to "undertake to prohibit, prevent and, if necessary, put a stop to any form of theft, pillage or misappropriation of, and any acts of vandalism directed against, cultural property...." Despite its wording, this obligation has been interpreted to apply only to prevent one's own military from engaging in looting and vandalism and not to preventing third parties from doing so.

An occupying power should work with the national authorities of the occupied country to preserve the occupied nation's cultural property (Article 5). The occupying power must "take the most necessary measures" to preserve cultural property that was damaged by military operations but only if the national authorities are not able to do so. Major drawbacks to this provision became evident, most significantly in that the obligation to preserve cultural property is limited to those cultural sites, monuments, and objects that were damaged during hostilities. There is no obligation to carry out preservation or conservation measures for cultural property that is damaged by some other means, such as through looting and vandalism. The Hague Convention seems most concerned with preventing an occupying power from interfering with the cultural, historical, and religious record of occupied territory and therefore requires preservation, which could become interference, under only these narrow circumstances. However, these limitations can produce a result that is inconsistent with the overall goals of the convention to preserve cultural property.

The First Protocol, also written in 1954, is concerned primarily with the status of movable cultural objects and essentially imposes four obligations. First, an occupying power is obligated to prevent the export from occupied territory of any movable cultural property. Second, any nation that is a party to the convention must take into its custody any illegally exported cultural property that is imported either directly from the occupied territory or indirectly through another nation. Third, at the close of hostilities, any state party must return cultural property to the competent authorities of the formerly occupied nation if the export from the occupied territory was in violation of the convention. Finally, any cultural property taken into custody during hostilities for the purpose of protecting it must also be returned at the end of hostilities.

The United States and United Kingdom signed the main convention (although not the First Protocol) in 1954, signifying their intention to ratify it. However, cold war tensions intervened, and even after the U.S. military withdrew its objections to ratification after the fall of the Soviet Union and after President Clinton transmitted the convention to the Senate in 1999, no further action toward ratification was taken until February of 2007, when the State Department included the convention on the treaty priority list submitted to the Senate Foreign Relations Committee. As yet, the Senate has not taken any action. In May 2004, the United Kingdom announced its intention to ratify the convention and both protocols, and in January 2008 it released draft legislation for public comment. This legislation, if adopted, will create a criminal offense as required by the Second Protocol, a criminal offense for dealing in cultural objects removed from occupied territory in violation of the First Protocol, and forfeiture mechanisms to recover cultural objects taken in violation of the First Protocol. In 2007, Germany became the first nation to adopt legislation implementing the First Protocol by prohibiting dealing in cultural objects illegally removed from occupied territory of another state party any time after 1967, the date when Germany ratified the First Protocol.

On the other hand, the United States and the United Kingdom accept and purport to follow those principles of the convention that are part of customary international law and they continue to be bound by the Hague Conventions of 1899 and 1907. Such actions as the construction of a military base on the historically and archaeologically significant site of Babylon seem to contravene provisions of the Hague Convention and likely violate international customary law as well.

The 1970 UNESCO Convention

The 1970 UNESCO Convention was written in response to the growth of the international art market in the years following World War II and the market's growing contribution to the theft and illegal export of cultural property, the looting of archaeological sites, and the dismemberment of other cultural monuments. The United States was one of the first market nations to ratify it, but today most of the significant market nations are party to the convention. Although the Senate voted unanimously to ratify the convention in 1972, United States implementing legislation, the Convention on Cultural Property Implementation Act (CPIA), was not passed until 1982, and it implements only two sections of the convention: Article 7(b) and Article 9.

Article 7(b) calls on those nations that are party to the convention "to prohibit the import of cultural property stolen from a museum or a religious or secular public monument or similar institution in another state party …, provided that such property is documented as appertaining to the inventory of that institution." The CPIA permits the Bureau of Immigration and Customs Enforcement (formerly U.S. Customs) to seize at the border any stolen cultural property that had been documented as part of the inventory of a museum or other public institution located in another nation that is a party to the convention without having to demonstrate that the importer knew that the property is stolen (19 U.S. Customs § 2607).

Unlike Article 7(b), which applies to all types of cultural objects, Article 9 applies only to archaeological and ethnological materials. Upon request from another state party, the CPIA allows the U.S. president to impose import restrictions on designated categories of archaeological and ethnological materials pursuant to either a bilateral agreement, which is negotiated between the United States and the other country, or an emergency action, in cases of crisis threats to the other country's cultural heritage. Such restrictions prevent the import into the United States of archaeological and ethnological material that left the country of origin after the imposition of the restrictions and that do not have an export license. Throughout the years of the sanctions imposed on Iraq after its invasion of Kuwait in 1990, Iraq could not request a bilateral agreement with the United States because the two nations did not have diplomatic relations, which are necessary for the submission of a request.

For the United States to enter into a bilateral agreement, four criteria must be demonstrated: first, that the other country's cultural patrimony is in jeopardy from pillage of archaeological or ethnological objects; second, that the other country has taken internal steps consistent with the convention (that is, the other country has undertaken education and law enforcement efforts to reduce pillage); third, that the United States's action will be taken as part of a multilateral effort; fourth, that imposing import restrictions would further the public interest in international exchange of cultural materials for scientific and educational purposes. There is also an exception to the third criterion (the multilateral requirement) if the United States's imposition of import controls would be of substantial benefit to preventing pillage even if other countries with a significant import trade in the same materials do not undertake similar import controls. Bilateral agreements last for a maximum of five years and may be renewed an unlimited number of times.

The U.S. president may also impose import restrictions unilaterally when a crisis situation in the requesting nation threatens its cultural patrimony. However, the other nation cannot bring a request for an emergency action; rather, it must first request a bilateral agreement and the same, lengthy process to determine whether the criteria for both a bilateral agreement and emergency action are satisfied is required. An emergency action lasts for a maximum of five years and may be renewed only one time for an additional three years.

With the exception of the United States, most nations that ratified the UNESCO Convention apply import controls across the board — that is, they prohibit the import into their country of any cultural objects that had been illegally exported or stolen from their country of origin. Canada is an example of this in that its statutory provision simply prohibits the import of illegally exported cultural objects from other state parties to the convention. Australia goes a step further in that it prohibits the import of all illegally exported cultural objects, even if the country of origin is not a party to the convention. Beginning in 2002, several additional market nations ratified the UNESCO Convention, including the United Kingdom, Japan, Denmark, Germany, and Switzerland.

As part of its ratification, the British Parliament enacted a new Dealing in Cultural Objects (Offences) Act 2003. The British legislation creates a new criminal offense for dealing in "tainted cultural objects." One commits this offense if he or she "dishonestly deals in a cultural object that is tainted, knowing or believing that the object is tainted." The statute defines a "tainted object" under the following circumstances: "A cultural object is tainted if, after the commencement of this Act (a) a person removes the object in a case falling within subsection (4) or he excavates the object, and (b) the removal or excavation constitutes an offence." Subsection 4 refers to objects removed from "a building or structure of historical, architectural or archaeological interest" or from an excavation. For purposes of the statute, it does not matter whether the illegal excavation or removal takes place in the United Kingdom or in another country or whether the law violated is a domestic or foreign law.

Switzerland also enacted implementing legislation that took effect in June 2005. The new Swiss legislation, the Federal Act on the International Transfer of Cultural Property, implements the UNESCO Convention in a manner that is closer to the United States' model by allowing the Swiss Federal Council to enter into agreements with other nations that are party to the UNESCO Convention to protect "cultural and foreign affairs interests and to secure cultural heritage." The Federal Council can also take additional measures when a "state's cultural heritage [is] jeopardized by exceptional events." Unlike the U.S. bilateral agreements, however, the Swiss agreements may last for an indefinite period of time and do not need to be renewed. It is reported that Switzerland has entered into agreements with Peru, Italy, Greece, and Egypt.

Laws of General Application

In addition to implementation of the 1970 UNESCO Convention, several other aspects of U.S. domestic law are relevant to the legal regime to prevent the importation of looted archaeological objects. Any objects stolen from the Iraq Museum and other cultural institutions in Iraq clearly constitute stolen property and as such implicate numerous legal doctrines. In addition to the CPIA prohibition on import of stolen cultural property, the National Stolen Property Act prohibits import of, possession of, and trading in any stolen property if its value exceeds (or the value of a shipment exceeds) $5,000. Anyone who knowingly receives, transports, or deals in such stolen cultural objects is liable to criminal prosecution under the National Stolen Property Act. The Customs statute also prohibits import of stolen property and property that is not properly declared upon entry into the United States.

A much more difficult problem is raised by the looting of archaeological sites. Looted objects may be particularly appealing to the international art market because their existence is undocumented and there is no record of their theft. It is therefore extremely difficult for law enforcement to trace such objects through normal methods and to establish their true origin. To combat this form of theft, many nations have enacted laws that vest ownership of undiscovered archaeological objects in the nation and thereby deny title to the looter and subsequent purchasers. These ownership laws apply to any objects discovered or excavated after the effective date of the statute. If an object is excavated (or looted) after this date and removed from the country without permission, then the object is stolen property and it retains this characterization even after it is brought to the United States. Anyone who knowingly transports, possesses, or transfers stolen property in interstate or international commerce, or intends to do so, violates the National Stolen Property Act. Depending on the factual circumstances and the proof available to the government, the stolen property may be seized and forfeited and the individual may be subject to criminal prosecution.

This doctrine was tested in the 2001 prosecution of the prominent New York antiquities dealer, Frederick Schultz. Until shortly before his indictment, Schultz was president of the National Association of Dealers in Ancient, Oriental and Primitive Art. Schultz was indicted on one count of conspiring to deal in antiquities stolen from Egypt in violation of Egypt's national ownership Law 117, which was enacted in 1983. The court examined the Egyptian law and held that it was a true ownership law, both because it plainly stated that it was and because it was internally enforced within Egypt. Iraq's declaration of national ownership dates to 1936, and so any archaeological objects removed without permission after this date are stolen property under U.S. law. The knowing import of such materials would violate the National Stolen Property Act and those handling such objects may be subject to prosecution. A British appellate court recently confronted this doctrine in the case *Iran v. Barakat*. The court held that Iran's antiquities law of 1979 created national ownership and that, if the necessary factual circumstances can be proven, Iran will be able to recover archaeological artifacts allegedly looted from the Jiroft region.

Laws Specific to Iraq

One unusual aspect of the legal regime as applied to looting in Iraq was that United Nations-mandated sanctions on the import of goods from Iraq had been in place since August 1990. In the United States, these sanctions were implemented through a Presidential Executive Order and were administrated by the Treasury Department's Office of Foreign Asset Controls. Archaeological and other cultural objects that were exported from Iraq after August 1990 were therefore already prohibited entry into the United States even before the second Gulf War began.

The considerable media attention that focused on the looting of Iraq, particularly the looting and vandalism at the museums, libraries, and archives in Baghdad, led to the enactment of several provisions unique to the Iraq situation. In anticipation of the lifting of the general trade sanctions, on May 22, 2003, the United Nations Security Council passed a resolution that included a specific provision for dealing with the cultural materials of Iraq (UNSCR 1483 ¶ 7). This provision states that the Security Council

> decides that all Member States shall take appropriate steps to facilitate the safe return to Iraqi institutions of Iraqi cultural property and other items of archaeological, historical, cultural, rare scientific, and religious importance illegally removed from the Iraq National Museum, the National Library, and other locations in Iraq since the adoption of resolution 661 (1990) of 6 August 1990, including by establishing a prohibition on trade in or transfer of such items and items with respect to which reasonable suspicion exists that they have been illegally removed, and calls upon the United Nations Educational, Scientific, and Cultural Organization, Interpol,

and other international organizations, as appropriate, to assist in the implementation of this paragraph.

Several of the market nations undertook particular legislative or administrative actions to implement this Security Council Resolution, as they are required to do under the United Nations Charter. For example, the European Union enacted Council Regulation No. 1210/2003, which, in paragraph 3, prohibits the import, export, or dealing in Iraqi cultural materials largely as defined in the United Nations Security Council Resolution if there is reasonable suspicion that the goods were "removed in breach of Iraq's laws and regulations." The United Kingdom enacted Statutory Instrument 2003 No. 1519, which prohibits the import or export of any illegally removed Iraqi cultural property. The dealing in any such items constitutes a criminal offense unless the individual "proves that he did not know and had no reason to suppose that the item in question was illegally removed Iraqi cultural property." The Swiss Federal Council enacted an Ordinance on Economic Measures of 28 May 2003, which imposed a ban that "covers importation, exportation and transit, as well as selling, marketing, dealing in, acquiring or otherwise transferring Iraqi cultural assets stolen in Iraq since 2 August 1990, removed against the will of the owner, or taken out of Iraq illegally. It includes cultural assets acquired through illegal excavations. Such assets are presumed to have been exported illegally if they can be proved to have been in the Republic of Iraq after 2 August 1990."

While the United States issued a general license on May 23, 2003, thereby lifting the sanctions on import of goods from Iraq, it included a "carve-out" so that the prohibition on import of or other transactions involving Iraqi cultural materials as described in the United Nations Security Council Resolution continued without any hiatus. In addition, on December 3, 2004, the Emergency Protection for Iraqi Cultural Antiquities Act was signed into law. This legislation allows the president to exercise his authority under the CPIA to impose import restrictions on any cultural materials, as defined in the United Nations Security Council Resolution (which is broader than the definition of archaeological and ethnological materials contained in the CPIA), illegally removed from Iraq after August 1990. As yet, however, the president has not exercised this authority. While many of these legal provisions in the United States and other nations are unique to the situation in Iraq, the rapid and relatively widespread implementation of these provisions demonstrates that the legal system can respond when there is sufficient public attention brought to the issue of archaeological looting and destruction of cultural heritage.

What Can Be Done

Although the United States signed the Hague Convention in 1954, no action toward ratification was taken until President Clinton transmitted it to the Senate in 1999. In February of 2007, the State Department included the convention on its list of treaties for consideration by the Senate Foreign Relations Committees, but, as yet, the Senate has not taken any action. Not under consideration at this time by the United States is the Second Protocol because it has not yet been reviewed by the Department of Defense and other executive agencies. Perhaps its most important provision is that the Second Protocol clarifies the criminal responsibility of individuals who violate its terms and requires nations to establish criminal offenses under their domestic law. The Second Protocol also narrows the circumstances in which the military necessity waiver would apply; it creates a system of enhanced protection for cultural property that meets certain criteria and it limits further the ability of an occupying power to interfere with the cultural and historical record of occupied territory. The Second Protocol did not come into effect until 2004 and none of the major parties to the current Iraq conflict have ratified it.

If the U.S. Senate votes to ratify the Convention, Congress will then be required to enact implementing legislation. It is likely this legislation would take the form of amendments to the Uniform Code of Military Justice. Ratification of the Hague Convention would clarify to the U.S. military its obligations to train and educate the troops about cultural heritage preservation. Ratification would require the U.S. military to maintain personnel who are equipped and trained to help in preservation efforts and would require the U.S. military to incorporate cultural heritage preservation priorities into the earliest stages of all its planning. It is to be hoped that the United States will follow the lead of the United Kingdom in ratifying not only the main Convention but also both protocols. This would provide even greater protection for cultural heritage during armed conflict.